## DEDICATION

To the survivors and their memories;
To Zalman Grinberg and Edward Herman,
   who did much for many;
And to those American soldiers who kept hope
   alive.

A Seven Stories Press First Edition
All rights reserved.
Copyright © 1997 by Robert L. Hilliard

Except as permitted under the Copyright Act of 1976, no part of this book may be reproduced or distributed in any form or by any means or stored in a data base or retrieval system without the prior written permission of the publisher.

Library of Congress Cataloguing-in-Publication Data
Hilliard, Robert L., 1925-
Surviving the Americans : the continued struggle of the Jews after liberation : a memoir / by Robert L. Hilliard.
     p. cm.
ISBN 1-888363-32-0
   1. Jews—Germany—History—1945- . 2. Jews—German (West)—History. 3. Holocaust survivors—Germany (West) 4. Germany (West)—Ethnic relations. 5. Germany (Terriory under Allied occupation, 1945-1955 : U.S. Zone)—Politics and government. 6. Hilliard, Robert L., 1925- . I. Title.
DS135.G332H55 1996
940.53' 1743—dc20                96-30277
                            CIP

10 9 8 7 6 5 4 3 2 1
Printed in the United States of America
Book design by Morgan Brilliant

# SURVIVING THE AMERICANS

## The Continued Struggle of the Jews
## After Liberation

by Robert L. Hilliard, Ph.D.

Seven Stories Press
New York

# TABLE OF CONTENTS

# Acknowledgments

I am grateful to Dan Simon, publisher, Moyra Davey, and Jon Gilbert of Seven Stories Press for making it possible for this story to be told in book form. I thank copy editor Elinor Nauen for her suggestions. I appreciate the encouragement of many to finally put down on paper what I have verbally recounted to them for years, especially my son Mark Verheyden-Hilliard, my daughter Mara Verheyden-Hilliard, and Mary Ellen Verheyden-Hilliard. Friends who provided encouragement and help include Regine Barshak and Mike Keith. I appreciate the assistance with photos, documents, and recollections from Miriam Schiff, Adele Green, Arnold Berman, Leonard Herman, Miriam Greenberg and Anthony DiBiase, and the proofreading suggestions of Carol Herman. I thank Eric Nooter, Bonnie Gurewitsch, and Krysia Fisher for help in locating photos; colleagues Burt Peretsky, Bill Daly, and Skip Sesling for their assistance, and Ursula Stone for German language corrections. Edward Herman, my letter-writing partner, has my special appreciation for his gathering of materials and documents, his remembrances, and for his enthusiasm and support, as does Carla Brooks Johnston for her ideas and encouragement. And I thank Miriam, Adele, and Edward, key figures in this account of the Holocaust survivors in post-war Germany, for their time and patience in checking the manuscript for accuracy.

My appreciation, too, to the survivors and GIs who shared with me, in 1945 and 1946, their experiences and feelings, which, along with notes, documents, letters and photos and my own recollections helped recreate the events and people of that period. Some reading this book who were at St. Ottilien, either as patients or as GIs who helped, might not recognize the author's name because not long after the war, when I began my professional career in the media, at first as a performer, I changed Robert Hilliard Levine to Robert L. Hilliard. An important purpose in writing this book is to keep the lessons of the Holocaust and its aftermath alive so that young people, like my nephew Zeke Martin, will hopefully not let it happen again.

# Introduction ⌒

"What's the difference between you Americans and the Nazis," a concentration camp survivor said to me, a U.S. soldier in U.S.-occupied Germany a few months after World War II had ended in Europe, "except that you don't have gas chambers!"

The war was over and the survivors of the camps had been freed. But the genocide that the Germans had begun did not end. The American Armed Forces who occupied Bavaria and part of Austria continued it for months after V-E Day, May 7, 1945. Genocide by neglect, some called it. Deliberate neglect, others suggested.

At the end of April almost all the camps had been opened and the prisoners who still lived were freed. General Dwight D. Eisenhower, Supreme Commander of the Allied Expeditionary Forces in Europe, had refused to order the advancing U.S. Army to liberate the camps and save the lives of tens and perhaps hundreds of thousands who were killed by the retreating German Army and government in the final weeks of the war. Nevertheless, the American soldiers who accidentally came upon the camps as they pursued the retreating Germans toward the Austrian and Czechoslovakian borders were so shocked by what they saw that they stopped and liberated the surviving prisoners. In the months following the end of the war, many of those who thought the defeat of the Nazis would release them from the living hell they had come to know under the German regime found themselves starved, raped and even shot by the same American forces that had freed them.

There weren't that many survivors to begin with. Jews, some non-Jewish communists and political dissenters, some priests and ministers whose integrity of belief prevented them from cooperating with the Nazis, some homosexuals and some Gypsies. Almost all the non-Jews joined the endless lines of caravans walking back to their homelands. The Jews just wandered. They had no place to go back to. Within a few weeks after the end of the war stories began filtering back from Poland, Latvia, Lithuania and other countries about pogroms against returning Jews almost as violent as those under Hitler. Many of the Jews who went back looking for surviving members of their families or who sought out their original homes and businesses—which had been seized and given to non-Jews—were shot or beaten to death in the streets of their former towns. The people in these countries continued to blame the Jews for the war and for their present deprivation and the destruction of their cities. People's attitudes don't necessarily change because they've lost a war or their leader isn't around anymore.

The survivors who stayed in Germany had to exist with few rights or opportunities; many were put in camps by the U.S. forces, surrounded by barbed wire, given little or no food or clothing, and no medicine. Because they had nothing else to wear, most had to continue to wear their striped camp uniforms and, in some cases, even the discarded uniforms of the hated SS troops.

The Jews had no choice. The United States Military Government (USMG) in Germany, which was put in charge of all displaced persons (D.P.s), including concentration camp survivors and slave laborers from other countries, required the D.P.s to declare their nationality in order to get food and housing entitlements. Once that was done, the MG required the D.P.s either to return on the next available transport to their original country or to become German residents. The Jews could do neither. Some, with the false papers that had saved them from the camps in the first place, continued to pose as non-Jews and tried to get jobs. Most were forced into the D.P. camps, many of which differed little from the conditions of the Nazi concentration camps.

At many camps the only food the survivors got was that smuggled in by individual American soldiers past the American Military Police, who had been ordered not to permit the bringing in of any unofficial supplies. In a few instances, the women were compelled to have sex with their American guards if the survivors wanted food and clothing.

Nothing was done, despite pleas from the survivors and from many individual U.S. soldiers to the U.S. military command, to the USMG, to Jewish organizations in the United States, to international relief organizations and to General Eisenhower at Supreme Headquarters Allied Expeditionary Forces (SHAEF) in Paris. After a few months, with thousands of survivors continuing to die from malnutrition and lack of medicine with which to help recover from years of debilitation, it seemed likely that those Jews who hadn't died from deliberate murder inside the concentration camps would soon die from starvation and disease outside of them.

It was then that two young army privates in the American occupation forces, who had attempted to help the survivors and been increasingly frustrated by what appeared to be a losing battle, wrote a letter that helped change the course of events. Surreptitiously written, printed in hundreds of copies and sent to friends and relatives for distribution throughout the United States, the nine-page document detailed the continuing horrors inflicted upon the survivors of the Holocaust and accused the American people of continued genocide. I was one of the young soldiers. E. Edward Herman was the other.

While we knew we risked retribution, including possible court-martial, we also knew that if something wasn't done soon, thousands of survivors would likely perish. We especially worried about the coming of winter, by then only several months away.

The absurdity of two privates challenging the policies and practices of the entire United States Army in Europe and its Commanding General, Dwight Eisenhower, did not occur to us at the time. Nevertheless, our letter was a factor in President Harry S Truman's ordering General Eisenhower, in what some considered a public reprimand, to change U.S. policy toward the survivors.

The front page of *The New York Times* on September 30, 1945, headlined the story: "PRESIDENT ORDERS EISENHOWER TO END NEW ABUSE OF JEWS / Likens Our Treatment to That of the Nazis / Conditions for Displaced in Reich Called Shocking."

The letter Edward Herman and I distributed, we were later told, reached President Truman, who was disturbed by what appeared to be outrageous allegations. Earlier, he had asked Earl G. Harrison, then on leave from his position as dean of the University of Pennsylvania Law School while serving as President Truman's representative to the Intergovernmental Committee on Refugees, to investigate and personally inspect the conditions of the D.P. camps in the

American occupation zone of Germany. Harrison's report stated, in part: "As matters now stand, we appear to be treating the Jews as the Nazis treated them except that we do not exterminate them. They are in concentration camps in large numbers under our own military guard instead of SS troops. One is led to wonder whether the German people, seeing this, are not supposing that we are following or at least condoning Nazi policy."

President Truman acted immediately following his receipt of Dean Harrison's report.

This is what this book is about: the survival of the survivors in an atmosphere of "genocide by neglect" under the American occupation forces in immediate post-World War II Germany.

Those who lived through the Holocaust encountered many problems in their struggle to stay alive after liberation: They were forced to establish their own hospital; they were subject to overt anti-Semitism by U.S. forces, including deliberate as well as accidental shootings and the breaking up of one camp's first Yom Kippur service following liberation; they saw special favors given by U.S. officers to known Nazis at the expense of Jewish survivors; they watched the appointment to civilian political positions by the U.S. military government of Nazis, including Bürgermeisters (mayors), who had held the same or comparable positions under Hitler; they saw how USMG officers fell under the control of their young German mistresses working as their secretaries and translators; they suffered as official orders from the U.S. military command rescinded sanctions and penalties on former active Nazis; they wondered at the lack of any serious attempt to reeducate the German public away from Nazi beliefs; and they were shocked by the tacit U.S.

support, as verified in Dean Harrison's report, of Nazi ideology.

This story revolves principally around the survivors' hospital at St. Ottilien, a church village not far from Landsberg in northern Bavaria. The hospital was set up by the survivors themselves because no medical facility was provided by the U.S. occupation forces. St. Ottilien was both a microcosm of and a focal point for the survivor camps throughout the U.S. zones in Germany and Austria.

A number of American officers and enlisted men did try to help the survivors at St. Ottilien. Most of these GIs were not career army men. Whether enlistees or draftees, most, it seemed, had come to Germany vowing to help defeat Nazism. Often, in their mutual commitment and endeavors, the usual officer-enlisted man protocol and relationship momentarily disappeared. That they put aside some of the traditional army practices in order to fight the legacy of Nazism was not surprising. I recall some names, but, unfortunately, not all. And as I write them down I am not certain that I remember the spellings correctly. Captain Otto Raymond, Chaplain Abraham Klausner, Captain Maxwell Kirchner, Chaplain Claude Bond, Lieutenant Jack Manheim, Lieutenant Albert Cusick, Captain I. Jacobson, Captain Nathan Nathanson, Lieutenant Mark Parker; and my enlisted-man buddies ranging from master sergeant to private: Ernest Belkin, Al Bergman, Robert Shor, Eli Isaacson, Max Miller, Morris Shapiro, Anthony DiBiase, Francis Kline, Sam Weisel, Robert Kingsbury and, most especially, E. Edward Herman. I apologize to those whose names have faded from my memory; their deeds and the events surrounding them, however, have been recorded from notes, documents and the remembrances of several eyewitnesses as accurately as the withering of time has permitted.

# Chapter 1 ～

## The Liberation Concert

On May 27, 1945, I was an American soldier, the editor of an army newspaper in Bavaria, Germany. I heard about a concert being given by and for concentration camp survivors at their just-established hospital at St. Ottilien, a church complex not far from Munich. It was a "liberation concert," to commemorate their liberation only one month earlier from the Nazi Holocaust. This would make an excellent feature story for my newspaper, the *2nd Wing Eagle*, I thought.

In itself, the idea of the survivors holding a concert so soon after their release from the death camps appeared to be an anomaly. In a way, it seemed almost frivolous. I would soon learn better.

It was a cool, not-quite-summer day, the chill of the Bavarian Alps stretching across the rolling hills and past the lakes north to Munich, when I drove to St. Ottilien. A narrow dirt road off the main route wound around several farm buildings, past a field of new grass, bushes and wild flowers, through a gate that marked off the boundaries of the church complex, to the edge of a broad green lawn and into a scene out of a Rene Clair movie.

I parked my jeep at the edge of the grass and stared. At the far end of the lawn was a stage several feet off the ground, made of nondescript, non-matching wooden boards and covered with a loosely stretched canopy of patched and sewn sheets and discarded parachute cloth. Rows of wooden chairs were set in front of the stage, In the aisles, on the chairs and on the grass, standing, sitting, walking, leaning, lying, were hundreds of stick figures, emaciated, pale, skeletal, expressionless, all dressed in the black and white striped uniforms of the concentration camps. They barely moved, and when they did it was in the flickering slow motion of early silent films.

For a moment I pictured myself sitting in my college dormitory room reading Dante's *Inferno*. For several minutes I just stared.

Then, off to the side, I saw other people. In an area separated from the survivors' quarters were dozens of men wearing the green-gray military uniforms of the German armed forces, walking about in the careless manner of the privileged, smoking cigarettes, some with bandaged limbs, some leaning on white-uniformed female nurses, the hands and arms of enlisted men shooting out and up in prompt salutes to the German officers and doctors who passed by. From a distance, it too looked like a slow-motion film, orchestrated for its sharp, precise, rhythmic movements.

Between these two scenes of victim and victimizer in a Dantean limbo where the winner was the loser and the loser the winner, was a high masonry wall that set off the main part of the complex with its church and living quarters, now occupied by the priests and nursing sisters and the German physicians whose otherwise secluded life was devoted to giving whatever physical and spiritual aid they could to the German soldiers. Some of the Germans, walking down to the far end of the dividing wall where it stopped at the edge of the dirt road, were able to look directly at the concentration camp survivors. But there was no indication on their faces that they saw them. Occupying the four buildings on this side of the wall were barely four hundred survivors. It had been only a month since they had been freed, following thirteen years of terror including the past six years of torture. They were without food, without clothing, without medical aid. Four hundred of them in the midst of their former captors and torturers who pretended as though they didn't exist. Four hundred of them, the remnants of millions. Four hundred of them, sick, starving, ragged, dying, on this late spring day in Bavaria, on this afternoon of May 27, 1945. And what were they doing? They were giving a concert!

Onto the stage men and women carried fiddles, horns, bass viols. Through the years in the camps, wood, string, metal parts of instruments had been smuggled, cared for and put together to create music, a link with what they remembered of a rational civilization. In some camps the Germans had provided instruments to designated groups of musicians who would greet new arrivals with music and play them on their unknowing way to the gas chambers. Now it was not a celebration of death, but of life. Now it was an announcement of their survival. One of the musicians walked slowly to the front of the stage. "This is our liberation concert," he said.

A liberation concert at which most of the liberated people were too weak to stand. A liberation concert at which most of the people still could not believe they were free. I got out of my jeep and walked down to the benches and sat among the people. Some of them looked at me; their eyes were hollow. I thought I saw in them a sense of gratefulness. After all, I was one of their liberators.

Or was that only what I wanted to see? Was it, rather, disappointment that in these first weeks of their liberation the aid and compassion they had expected from us Americans was not forthcoming? Or was it a silent plea to give them the help they needed to survive a little longer? Perhaps I only imagined these feelings and I really saw nothing; perhaps the Holocaust had left their souls, like their eyes, empty.

The musicians played Mahler, Mendelssohn and others whose music had been forbidden for years. A concert of life and a concert of death. The sounds of the music welled into anguish. The movements and faces of the musicians were cramped, tight, fearful, as if they could not believe there was room to move a bow or air in which to blow a note, as if they momentarily expected guns and clubs to tear apart what, after so many years, must have felt to them only a dream.

When the concert ended many people were crying, few more openly than I. Many continued to sit or lie as they had been, their faces and bodies unmoving. A man in the front row came to the stage. He was thin, erect, of medium height, perhaps in his early 40s. He walked more firmly and seemed stronger than the others.

"I am Dr. Zalman Grinberg," he said, "I am head doctor at this hospital for political ex-prisoners."

It was an appropriate term, "political ex-prisoners." Although most of the survivors at St. Ottilien were Jews, some were not, including a few communists and clergy who had been political dissidents.

"Today is our liberation concert," Dr. Grinberg continued. "I speak in German because we have here people from many countries and with many languages. German has become for us a common tongue." Dr. Grinberg spoke softly and slowly. The passion was inside. It was more than a speech. It was a chronicle of tragedy. It was a canticle for the dead. It was a statement of martyrdom. It was a reminder that there could never be a forgetting. Those who for years had cried only on the inside could now cry openly.

This is the complete text of the speech delivered by Zalman Grinberg, M.D., head doctor of the hospital for political ex-prisoners in Germany, at the liberation concert in St. Ottilien on May 27, 1945:

"Four hundred and twenty Jews, the last representatives of the European Jews, after the most difficult period of suffering ever conceived, are now here in the hospital of St. Ottilien. These people are among the few survivors of the venerable old Jewish communities of Europe. Budapest and Prague, Warsaw, Kovno and Saloniki are represented here.

"Millions of members of these same communities have been annihilated. What is the logic of fate to let us, then, live? We belong in the common graves of those shot in Kharkow, Lublin and Kovno; we belong to the millions gassed and burnt in Auschwitz and Birkenau; we belong to the tens of thousands who died under the strain of the hardest labor; we belong to those tormented by milliards of lice, the mud, starvation, the cold of Lodz, Kielce, Buchenwald, Dachau, Landshut, Utting, Kaufering, Landsberg and Leonsberg. We belong to those who were gassed, hung, tortured, starved, worked and tormented to death in the concentration camps. We belong to the army of nine million fallen under the heel of this expertly organized and cunningly prepared system of murder. We are not alive—we are still dead!

"Nevertheless, there is a purpose in my address here today.

We act as delegates of millions of victims to tell all mankind, to proclaim all over the world how cruel people may become, what brutal hellishness is concealed within a human being, and what a triumphant record of crime and murder has been achieved by the nation of Hegel and Kant, Schiller and Goethe, Beethoven and Schopenhauer.

"Each one of us has had a different road of torture. During the past six years, almost all of the three and a half million Polish Jews have been lost. There remain perhaps ten thousand out of three hundred and fifty thousand Lithuanian Jews. Ninety-five percent of the Hungarian Jews have been annihilated.

"Yes, the road of torture is different. One led via Warsaw and Auschwitz to Upper Bavaria; another from Budapest via Auschwitz to Upper Bavaria; a third from Kovno-Stutthof to Upper Bavaria; still another form Lodz to Sachsenhausen, from Sachsenhausen to Belsen, from Belsen to Leonsberg, from Leonsberg to Kaufering.

"Different is the road, various are the stations of torture, unlike is the space of time—but together they form one common red thread of blood, torture, torment, humiliation—and violent death.

"In order to give you a slight intimation of what we went through, what we saw, and why we are still under the relentless pressure of the experiences of the last few years, I will try to give you a brief account of the stations of torture I personally passed during this time.

"Kovno, Saturday, June 21, 1941. The peaceful life is running its usual course.

"Kovno, Sunday, June 22, 1941. That night our sleep is disturbed by some kind of detonations. At first we take it for military maneuvering. However, we learn the next morning that Germany has attacked the Soviet Union without a declaration of war. Fighting is already going on at the frontiers, which caused anxiety, apprehension and excitement among all classes and all nationalities of the population. The German army approaches Kovno and takes the town. However, we are far behind the fighting zone and indeed glad that we avoided the menace of being caught between the firing lines. We expect little trouble.

"We know indeed that we shall be deprived of a certain amount of our civil rights, but we are almost secure in our hope that we shall survive this war together with our wives, children, parents and relatives. This hope was short-lived, for an announcement is heard through the radio that for every German soldier killed a hundred Jews would be shot! Simultaneously, a Lithuanian mob is organized under German leadership, and the worst kind of massacre imaginable is begun. Babes in arms were shot; ears, noses and fingers cut off; the bellies of young women slit—the devil celebrated his greatest triumph. The little homes in the suburbs of Kovno were flooded with blood. Men were brought in groups to the Seventh and Ninth Forts of Kovno and there machine-gunned. Women were tormented, violated and shot. This is not fiction, but true fact. It is all related by witnesses who succeeded in escaping from the death forts.

"Thousands lost their lives at the Seventh and Ninth Forts in this manner, but gradually the massacre died down. We lulled ourselves into a sense of false security by considering all this as merely an unfortunate incident of war, and again dared to hope that the survivors would be able to live in bearable conditions now. In the meantime, a civil government was established in Kovno and we thought that law and order would be the rule again.

"However, the first order issued by SA-Brigadeführer Cramer, the newly appointed commissioner of the town, read that all Jews must, under threat of the death penalty, bear on the breast and on the back a yellow star; that the Jews were not allowed to walk on the sidewalks, the gutter alone remaining for that purpose.

"We could do naught but bear this humiliation and hope that somehow this war would be soon over and this nightmare would end.

"Order No. 2 of SA-Brigadeführer Cramer read that the total Jewish population of Kovno had until August 15 to move to a little suburb of the town, and that after August 15, all Jews found outside the borders of the ghetto would be shot. Once more we are disillusioned and hopes fade. Twenty-six thousand persons from all parts of town, and by every means available, start moving to the ghetto in Viliampole. Up until the 15th of August there is one continuous caravan of men and women moving to their new homes.

"One square meter of dwelling space is allowed per person. Three square feet! But we ignore the lack of space, the dirt and squalor, and try to be content having our wives and children with us. We do not know how we are going to feed ourselves or our families, how we are going to clothe ourselves, how we are going to find warmth. We soon learn, though, to forget the future, to think about the present day only. We become hardhearted, our false illusions will only make us more bitter in the end. Our sole hope was that the most difficult part was now over, and that here in the ghetto we would be able to carry on some sort of existence. Around the ghetto a fence of barbed wire is built. A guard with fixed bayonets is stationed. We are imprisoned!

"Within the ghetto an administration must be established and a board of elders is formed. Venerable, well-known Dr. Elkes becomes the leader of this tragic community. A ghetto police is created, and various offices of administration are organized. We endeavor to create tolerable conditions by mutual help and organization. A hospital is established, with all the doctors bringing their instruments and medicines. Sanitary measures are taken throughout the ghetto to prevent epidemics. Ten cows that remained in the ghetto are put under the control of the board of elders to secure milk for the young ones. Everything was equally distributed, everyone bore his share of the suffering, for is it not true that shared suffering is milder suffering? During this period of feverish organization, the Third Police Company, under the command of a Captain Tornbaum, moved into the ghetto. Every house was searched, and all valuables were taken from us. This was an official plundering sanctioned by the state!

"You soon learn that property has, after all, no value, and you give all you think valuable to the intruders voluntarily. The Germans behave brutally in order to intimidate the population. Men, women and children are beaten cruelly. There is shooting on a large scale. The groans of wounded men and the cries of despairing women are heard all over the ghetto. Trucks are used to carry away the loot. This action continues for a full week.

"One now believes that the devil would be satisfied after you have thrown into his greedy throat silver, gold, wedding rings, furs, fabrics and linen. It is calm one day, and perhaps the crisis has passed. Now that we are poor, they should leave us in peace. But, in keeping with Nazi policy, this was not the case. The new orders are that our ten cows are to be delivered to the authorities, our children remaining without milk. That all valuables remaining should be delivered voluntarily. This is done, for we want to display our goodwill, we do not want to provoke the devil—we want to save our lives!

"Nevertheless, on October 4, one part of the ghetto is surrounded by heavily armed soldiers. The inhabitants of that section are driven to the street and there a part is picked at random, driven to the Ninth Fort and murdered!

"The hospital, our only means of caring for the sick and wounded, is locked and set afire. The patients, the doctors and the nurses are victims of this sadism.

"I am one of those supposedly fortunate ones who were allowed to join the other part of the ghetto. Even now I can see the blazing hospital. It seems like a bad dream, but, alas, it was true!

"I now remained without shelter for my wife and little child in another part of the ghetto; but fortunately I soon obtained lodging and some help. For the next twenty-four days nothing of importance happened and it seems as if the beast had left us to our lot. We were sure all the trouble was over; that they had merely wanted to reduce the population of the ghetto and accomplished it in this cruel way.

"On the 28th of October another edict was issued: All the population of the ghetto—healthy, ill, young, old—must be present at a certain place. Then began a game of chance—amusement for the Germans present, a game of life or death for those of the ghetto. Herr Rauca, a representative of the Gestapo in

Kovno, arrives, and as the columns of twenty-four thousand souls pass by him, he sends one part to the right, the other part to the left. The people are puzzled as to which side they should choose, for they still do not realize the significance of the situation.

"This procedure, which looks so much like the driving of cattle to market, goes on all day. In brief, the ten thousand eight hundred people who were sent to the right side were massacred at the Ninth Fort the following morning.

"The population of the ghetto is further diminished, and there is indeed more space for the survivors. However, there is no longer room for illusion, and we are all in a mood of deepest depression, sorrow and mourning.

"Once more the Nazi promises. SA-Hauptsturmführer Jordan arrives and declares to the board of elders: 'You have nothing to be afraid of in the future; you will work and live; you will work for the German Wehrmacht, and we will take care of you!' With that he throws 10,000 marks on the table and states that this was the first payment to the ghetto for the work they will do.

"But nobody trusts him; experience has made us suspicious. However, the coming months and years proved him to be accurate. Life in the ghetto became hard, everyone being forced to fulfill extreme physical labor.

"Although the ghetto was raided continually, there were no actions of great importance—until March 27, 1944. On this day the camp (the ghetto was now a concentration camp) was raided by the SS in a brutal hunt for children up to the age of 13.

"Like hunted and wounded animals, the children were thrown into the trucks of the SS. I can still see the heartrending scenes. I see mothers clinging to their children, I see mothers covering their children with their bodies, so that they may be shot instead of the children. I see the whole camp crying, the tears of innocent children, the wild despair of all, the sight of children being torn from their parents' arms.

"In the meantime, the SS is deploying in cars and motorcycles throughout the whole camp, shooting and fighting their gigantic battle—the battle against children!

" 'Give us your children! Are there any children here? Where did you hide your children?' I can hear it even now. Everyone is going wild trying to hide their children: in barrels, in the cellar, in the garret, in bedclothes! Some parents poison their children and then commit suicide!

"On the 29th of March the concentration camp of Kovno is empty of children. A few of the parents succeeded in hiding their little ones, but they must be kept hidden, since officially there are no children in the camp.

"July 12 came, and with the successful Russian offensive, the Soviet armies approached Kovno. The commander of the camp, SS-Obersturmbannführer Goecke declared that the camp must be evacuated and that there was no reason to fear; we were going to Germany and would be treated well there. We would go to and be with our families at the newly established concentration camp of Stutthof, near Danzig.

"They very graciously allowed us to take some things of value along because we would need them in Germany. The closer the front approached, the more we were promised!

"Those who did not trust those promises tried to escape through the fence of barbed wire. Some of these people were shot in flight, some got through to—no one knows! Some tried to hide themselves in the hope that at the rate the Russians were going they would soon be there. Working at night some of the people built hiding places and remained there. But their work was for naught—the Gestapo was too smart. The armed troops came into camp, blew up houses, set them afire, exploded grenades, fired small arms, and these people crept from their holes like frightened mice. Columns were quickly formed, brought to the railway station and shipped to Tiegenhof.

"When we arrived at Tiegenhof, our old SS guards are replaced by new troops of the Sturmführer. An order is immediately issued that all women and the rest of the children will be separated from the men and sent to a different place. The women weep, taking leave of their husbands, the children are crying bitterly. Thus all promises once again prove to be lies.

"The Jewish elder, the venerable Dr. Elkes, has the courage to approach an SS-Obersturmführer and ask him the reason why we were separated, despite the promises that had been given in Kovno. The brave Obersturmführer gives the 65-year-old doctor a box on the ears that is a clear reply. Dr. Elkes kisses his wife and takes leave of her. My wife is weeping and reproaching me because I did not listen to her advice and commit suicide rather than be evacuated to this new camp. I beg her to just wait and hope. Perhaps we would someday see each other again. As we were exchanging this last goodbye an SS-man approached and chased away my wife and all the other women who were seeing their husbands for what would be perhaps the last time.

"We were driven to wagons and locked up. We grew numb;

the blood in our veins almost stopped circulating. We were in a state of the greatest despair.

"It was clear to us that our women had started their last walk. It was clear to us that we in turn were going to our deaths. Our only wish—to die together with our loved ones—had been refused.

"Three long days and nights we were dragged through Germany in these dark wagons. We did not know our destination, but we did know that Jews from France, Belgium and Holland had been brought to Kovno and annihilated. We sat apathetic in our wagons and did not touch the meager food we had.

"Finally, we arrived at an unknown place and were ordered to get out. With anxious hearts we left the wagons. Were we brought here for labor, or was our last hour at hand? SS men formed us into columns of five each. There appeared Obersturmführer Foerster who had led the war against the children in Schaulen.

"A bad omen! Black clouds cover the sky and it begins to rain. This rain accompanies us to our new home. A camp only half ready. There are little tents for us to live in. Everything we possess is taken from us; even the photos of our families, passports and other documents are destroyed. It is explained to us that we have no rights whatsoever. 'If the bread of Dachau you eat from this moment on and if your rotten Jewish lives are of any value to you, you filthy pigs, you will have to obey blindly; otherwise you will perish much sooner than you can guess.' Thus spoke the famous Oberscharführer Kirsch. The destiny of we two thousand men is in the hands of Kirsch. Daily, Kirsch beats the old people cruelly, Kirsch ill-treats the youngsters, Kirsch picks out certain people from the ranks and compels them to bathe in the mire of the latrines. Kirsch governs the world of these two thousand men. Kirsch is the god and the ruler. Boys under 16 years of age are shipped to Auschwitz. The rest go daily the long way to the Moll factory. The Moll factory means twelve hours daily of the hardest labor in concrete and cement. Moll is terror, Moll is death! Day shift Moll, night shift Moll! Moll without interruption. Columns march to Moll, columns return from Moll. The people get thinner, food rations smaller. Three hundred grams of bread and watery soup. They begin to treat us in an even more brutal way. Fifty to sixty men die everyday. Sixty to eighty percent of those who had come to Kaufering lost their lives there. Those who are unable to work any more—starving, tortured by lice—are transferred to Camp 4, where they soon die.

"Many commanders come and go, each worse and more bestial than the other. We hear that on one front after another, Germany is suffering defeat, but there seems to be no change on our front. Those in charge of the camp have no scruples and do not hesitate in their brutality, even up to the last moment. Himmler himself ordered on April 14, 1945, that no prisoners should fall into Allied hands. We were to be evacuated to the Tyrol. The commandant of the camp declared publicly that we were going to be brought to Switzerland to be taken care of by the International Red Cross. One more lie! We learned later that the Red Cross knew nothing of such a plan. The truth is that we are to be annihilated. But fortunately Herr Himmler was no longer able to decide our destiny. The liberators had come earlier than those "gentlemen" had calculated.

"Partly on account of our long marches, previous treatment and being for a time within the fighting lines, we are still suffering heavy losses. Even in this hospital, where the people are no longer under the Nazi yoke, the Nazi regime demands new victims every day. We have thirty-five people buried in the cemetery here now!

"We have met here today to celebrate our liberation; but at the same time it is a day of mourning for us. Because every clear and joyful day at present or that may be in the future is overshadowed by the tragic events of the past years. One percent survived to see the liberation, and of these, ninety-nine percent are very ill. Are we able to enjoy this day? Are we able to celebrate?

"Hitler has lost every battle on every front except the battle against defenseless and unarmed men, women and children. He won the war against the Jews of Europe. He carried out this war with the help of the German nation.

"However, we do not want revenge. If we took vengeance, it would mean we would fall to the depths of ethics and morals the German nation has been in these past ten years.

"We are not able to slaughter women and children! We are not able to burn millions of people! We are not able to starve hundreds of thousands!

"We are free now, but we do not know how, or with what, to begin our free yet unfortunate lives. It seems to us that for the present mankind does not understand what we have gone through and experienced during this period. And it seems to us that we shall not be understood in the future.

"We unlearned to laugh; we cannot cry anymore; we do not understand our freedom: probably because we are still among our dead comrades!

"Let us rise and stand in silence to commemorate our dead!"

# Chapter 2 ᨞

## THE SURVIVORS

I first came across concentration camp survivors when the Second Air Disarmament Wing of the Army's Ninth Air Corps, to which I was assigned near the end of the war, arrived at a former German Luftwaffe training base on the outskirts of Kaufbeuren, about fifty miles southwest of Munich. The Second Air Disarmament Wing was a non-combat unit established to supervise the dismantling of the German Air Force, and included the search for and seizure of German inventions that might be of use to the U.S. Armed Forces. Among the items we found were new jet propulsion planes, advanced radar equipment and a prototype of the "flying wing," which the U.S. adapted into its own type of postwar streamlined jet aircraft.

The Second Wing was top-heavy with officers: about sixty for only three hundred and sixty enlisted men. The latter fell into three main categories: those who had spent most of the war in Air Corps units in England; rebels and misfits who had served time in U.S. Army prisons and detention camps for crimes ranging from theft to being AWOL (Absent Without Leave) to being disrespectful to officers who had ethnically, racially or religiously insulted them; and wounded ex-infantrymen whose injuries were not serious enough to send them back to the States, but serious enough to preclude their being sent back to their combat units, resulting in "limited assignment" duties in non-combat outfits such as the Second Wing. I was in the third group; my wounds in the Battle of the Bulge kept me from rejoining my Second Infantry Division company for the push to the Rhine River, but didn't warrant my returning to the States.

Because I had studied German and French in high school and had completed two years of college when I went into the service, the personnel officer of the Second Wing first put me into the Intelligence Office, ostensibly as a translator. What is most significant about this assignment was that my barely conversational German-language skills highlighted the paucity of preparation by the American military for conduct of its postwar occupation duties.

My first assignment—it was May 12, 1945—was to accompany an officer to a building in Kaufbeuren that had been a movie theater, to determine whether it should be requisitioned for the army's Special Services division. The Second Wing had what was called a Section 8 authorization, which gave the Wing the power to confiscate any material or property in Germany for U.S. Army use. While the officers of the Second Wing did, in fact, fulfill their duty to do this, some went a bit further. A number of officers used this authority to obtain and send home furs, cameras, medical instruments and other goods that the Germans had either manufactured or stolen from the countries they had occupied. In fact, the Second Wing became known as the army's "souvenir-hunting outfit."

The movie theater owner begged and pleaded that we allow him to retain his establishment. His pleas were heartrending. He told us that he had been an active anti-Nazi, despised Hitler and had opposed National Socialism in every way. With some misgivings, we took over the building, anyway. Several hours later, while going over documents that had been left in his office, we found that our misgivings were misplaced. His papers indicated that he had given countless contributions to the Nazi party and Nazi causes. It was my first of many lessons in how the Germans learned quickly to ingratiate themselves with the American conquerors; those who were the worst criminals usually were the first and most emphatic to deny it.

I also learned that day, from some of the documents we found in the theater, something that would be revealed in greater detail to the world in the ensuing months. Kaufbeuren had been the location during the war of a Children's Hospital that, in reality, was used for biological experiments of the most bizarre and cruel nature by German physicians on children taken there from various concentration camps. There was no evidence at that time that any of the children who had been brought to the hospital were still alive. I saw none in the town.

Occasionally I did see small groups of persons on the periphery of the city. Their emaciated bodies, shaved heads and ill-fitting clothing, which didn't completely cover their concentration camp uniforms, made it clear they were survivors of the Holocaust. I rarely saw a child among them.

We sometimes saw survivors along the roads between cities, skeletons in striped pajamas with torn rags wrapped around their feet, wandering through the countryside trying to find something to eat, a place to sleep and safety from the German populace that seemed intent on completing Hitler's "final solution." When there were no American soldiers around, the Germans would beat them, sometimes to death. Some were simply shot. There weren't many in that part of Bavaria who survived the camps, perhaps just a few thousand.

For the displaced persons who were not Jews, the slave laborers who had not been designated for extermination in the camps, it was a little different. They could go home. They had homes to return to. I saw many of these refugees moving toward their homes in eastern Europe, from where most had been taken as prisoners to work in Germany. Each day the lines grew longer and wider. Highways, streets, lanes, paths jammed with walking people, carrying small boxes, bundles, stuffed pillowcases, reminiscent of the Hollywood movies about the Depression of the 1930s that showed migrants carrying all their belongings wrapped in a cloth tied to the end of a stick.

At first I saw what seemed like large groups of these refugees. As time went on, they grew even larger. They came from everywhere and were going everywhere. There was no real sense of the vast numbers of displaced persons on the roads, until one saw them outside of the cities. In the cities they blended in with the other people on the streets, and except for the bundles they carried, it was difficult to tell that they didn't live there or that they were only passing through. At the edge of the cities, however, they converged, the straggling individuals and groups coming together from many city streets into a continuously moving mass on the highways.

Army vehicles tried to keep part of each road clear for trucks, jeeps and military automobiles, the latter mostly touring cars with senior officers and sports cars with junior officers. No civilians were allowed to ride unless on official business, and the soldiers in the back seats of jeeps and in the rear of trucks constantly pushed away hands grasping for a hold. The few civilian vehicles on the road were mostly old diesel trucks, creaking and chugging. They were filled to overflowing with refugees, people standing on the roof of the cab, sitting on fenders, lying across the hood, hanging on to any piece of wood or metal along the back or the sides, making triangles of their bodies with their feet hunched up into some crevice on the truck so that they wouldn't fall off, or simply hanging on, their feet dangling below, for as long as their arms could keep them there, and then falling off to join the walkers. Each time someone on a truck jumped or fell, someone on the road leaped up to take that place. The trucks couldn't move more than ten miles an hour, at best.

Almost everyone carried something: a tattered suitcase, a cardboard box tied with a string, a paper bag or the inevitable stuffed cloth with its four corners tied around the end of a stick. A few had their goods piled into baby carriages or onto makeshift carts for which they had somehow found wood, nails and wheels. Some carried nothing.

Many people were carried, too: babies in arms or older children who could go no farther on their own feet, spread-eagled across the chest or back of an adult who would rather make a few more miles even with the additional burden than stop to rest. A few very old or sick adults were helped limping along the road by an adult on each side, half-dragged, half-carried. Some of the baby carriages and carts had the sick and old as passengers, the sight as ludicrous as it was sad, the large adult head and arms preposterously sticking out and the body hunched over so that the knees almost touched the chin. Some of the people being carried piggyback were not children, but old men and women.

Almost all their clothes were tattered. If it hadn't been close to summer they would have frozen. Those who started out with shoes found that after fifty or a hundred or two hundred miles, the shoes became strands of flapping leather, to be stuffed with newspapers, then tied together with strips of rags, then discarded entirely. Many walked with nothing more than pieces of cloth wrapped around their feet. Others went barefoot. Old men and women walked slowly along the shoulder of the road, giving the younger, firmer walkers a chance to pass. Small children dashed in and out of the lines, those with a parent never losing sight of them, those without parents seeking an adult to latch on to, hoping for help and security at least on the march, until they got back to their hometowns to look for a parent or other relative who might still be alive. Older youths in their late teens and early 20s also dashed in and out of the lines, sometimes walking briskly ahead, sometimes running after a truck, trying to climb on to cover a few miles more quickly, sometimes looking for a youth their own age for a friendship that might be close for the next few days or weeks, but which would be abandoned when they came to divergent roads leading to different countries and cities, sometimes finding someone to walk hand-in-hand with more slowly and occasionally into a patch of thick grass or bushes off to the side of the road.

There was no schedule, no pace. The lines were never-ending, and anyone who slowed down or stopped in some town along the way or camped by the road or took time to rest in a field merely

joined what was an identical line of marchers whenever they resumed walking.

The lines never stopped. Even at night, when those who were
tired went a few feet off the road looking for the shelter of a tree or
the softness of thick grass or with luck an abandoned barn, and
slept for a few hours, the line continued.

They never seemed to eat, although occasionally people
pulled what looked like a biscuit or a piece of bread from a pocket
and munched on it as they walked along. Those who had D.P. identity cards stopped in the cities where they heard there might be a
sympathetic officer who might give them their quota of food, which
they stuffed inside pockets or paper sacks and ate as they resumed
their march. Others looked vainly for fields that might yield anything edible: roots or weeds or stems for soup, the remains of a
carrot or turnip patch. There were no farms or gardens with food
for the taking. Many of the fields were devastated, blackened by
bombing. Others had been stripped by their German owners or
townspeople when, toward the end of the war, it became clear that
food would be the most precious and scarce item. Anything left
had long been picked over by the D.P.s who began returning home
immediately after their city or factory or camp was liberated.

Sometimes clusters of people rested alongside the road, finding a common bond in conversation, seeking to reassure each other
that their return home would be successful. As might be expected,
those from the same country or the same city would establish a
bond and walk, stop, talk and move together in distinct groups.

Many people spent the hot days sitting or lying or sleeping,
resuming their march at night. Often one saw a woman with one

breast pulled out and over the top of a dress, snuggled into the face of a nursing baby, and one wondered where, in a hungry mother, the milk could come from. Maybe just being next to a warm body was, for the moment, enough sustenance for the baby.

When it rained nothing changed. A few more people went off the road looking for thick-branched trees under which to wait until the rain stopped. Most people continued to walk, their only acknowledgment of the rain a piece of cardboard or paper or cloth held up over their heads with one hand if they didn't need both hands to carry their belongings or give assistance to another person.

They moved virtually without sound. It was as if it took all of their energy to put one foot in front of the other, and their bodies shuffled, dipped forward, then bent back in a rhythmical bouncing motion, concentrating on each step, each movement isolating each person, who was, at the same time, part of a flowing pattern of mechanical unison that seemed to mark the whole line of people.

The walkers stayed mostly on the right side of the road, moving to the east. No one came west, into Germany, except for a few Germans who had been visiting relatives in nearby towns and some German soldiers returning from the eastern front, still in uniform.

Army vehicles used the left side of the road, weaving in and out of patches of marchers, speeding up when the road ahead was clear, slowing down and edging into the lines of walkers and civilian trucks when a vehicle came by from the opposite direction.

It would be months before the lines of refugees began to thin out and then finally disappear.

My military assignment soon changed in such a way that I was able not only to make contact and talk with survivors, but to work closely with them in their attempts to stay alive. Most of us enlisted men in the Second Wing had chips on our shoulders, either from a belief that as ex-infantrymen with Purple Hearts we should have been sent home or from a strong feeling of rebellion against authority, abusive and otherwise. We felt that nothing catastrophic could be done to us if we no longer jumped through the hoops of army authority. The war was over and the worst couldn't happen anymore: assignment to an infantry unit on the front lines. Although the war against Japan was still going on, we couldn't conceive—mistakenly for some of us, as it turned out—of being sent to the Pacific Theater of Operations. While I was eager to return home and resume my interrupted college education, I was happy, like most of the others, to be out of combat, and I was resigned to serving in the occupation forces until I became eligible for discharge.

The major in charge of personnel, who, we were told, had spent the entire war at an Air Corps base in England, regarded us with what seemed like a mixture of apprehension, fear, condescension and sympathy. Few of us had the special skills, at least as listed on our army records, required for most of the air disarmament jobs, and he let us request the jobs we wanted when at all possible. I had worked on my college newspaper, had been a part-time reporter and feature writer for several newspapers before entering the service and had some thoughts of perhaps one day becoming a journalist. This seemed like a good opportunity.

The major agreed to my proposal. "As soon as we get a Special Services officer, you can start a newspaper," he assured me. In the meantime he assigned me to the Intelligence Office.

Captain Nathan Nathanson arrived a couple of weeks later,

dressed in a chocolate brown uniform with flared pants, wide-lapel Eisenhower jacket and a tan silk tie, all custom-made by a German tailor.

"You're starting a newspaper, boychik, so start a newspaper."

Nate Nathanson appeared to be in his late 20s or early 30s and told us that before the war he had operated a boutique in Los Angeles that catered to the film colony. He seemed to miss the glamour he had apparently known back home, and we assumed he was making up for that, at least in part, by wearing made-to-order high-fashion uniforms, by going to individual homes in Kaufbeuren until he found an attractive and available woman whose expectations of cigarettes, food and silk stockings from an American officer made her an eager part of his harem, and by selling grasping German businessmen nonexistent war surplus equipment in exchange for money or goods that the Germans had probably stolen from other countries anyway. Although with a twinge of guilt, we couldn't help but envy and admire Nate. After the war, when I read *Catch-22*, with its wheeler-dealers, I wondered whether Joseph Heller, unbeknownst to me, also had been stationed at the Kaufbeuren air base.

Captain Nathanson gave me a free hand with the newspaper, including an assistant editor, Anthony DiBiase, motor pool privileges and an off-base pass to go anywhere at anytime to cover a story. I reported directly to Special Service Officer Lieutenant Mark Parker. Later on, when I used these privileges to aid survivors, Nathanson and Parker were supportive and became involved in their welfare.

It was shortly after I began editing the *2nd Wing Eagle* that I heard reports that in the church village of St. Ottilien, not far from Landsberg—in which prison Adolf Hitler had written *Mein Kampf*— a group of survivors had set up a hospital. They had emerged alive from Dachau and Buchenwald believing that the victorious Allied armies, especially that of the United States, would make a special effort to help them recover from their season in hell. They were doomed to bitter disappointment. The survivors received no official assistance from either the U.S. Army or U.S. Military Government officers who had been assigned to govern the towns that had come under American control. The survivors were left to shift for themselves, their only help coming from individual American soldiers they encountered on their wanderings out of and away from the concentration camps. They were liberated, but their struggle for survival continued.

# Chapter 3 ～

## DR. GRINBERG

Perhaps I should have felt elation and excitement on May 27, 1945, at St. Ottilien, when the remnants of the six million Jews who survived the German Holocaust under the eyes of a willing world held their liberation concert.

But I felt only desperation: the pain of those starving, ragged, sick, dying bodies.

Perhaps I should have thought of that day as an important moment in history, a rebirth of a people literally out of the ashes, the start of a new, important step forward in human progress. A liberation of people from the past, a new parting of the waters, one phase over, another beginning. Centuries later, maybe, historians might link that day to subsequent events and see its importance. But to those present it was neither a time of reflection nor of anticipation, but simply one of survival.

Were all great happenings of history merely unremarkable moments of transition for the people who made them and saw them?

History was not for watching but for doing, I decided, and I wondered how I could get some food, clothing and medicine to these few survivors before they too died. This was not a decision of conscious altruism or deliberate heroics. It came out of my own past, that of a kid growing up on the streets of Brooklyn during the Depression of the 1930s. I was lucky. Although both my parents had been immigrants from Europe, with little education, they had the fervor of most immigrants to make their children's lives better than their own. Having lost all the money they had made during the Roaring Twenties, my father and mother operated a small mom-and-pop retail bakery in the Bay Ridge-Sunset section of Brooklyn. The location is important because it helps explain my early experiences that influenced my wanting to help the people of St. Ottilien. The store was right across from one of the largest Catholic churches in New York, Our Lady of Perpetual Help, and on the opposite corner, in storefronts, were the headquarters of two of the most popular phenomena of the mid- and late-1930s: *The Tablet*, a right-wing Catholic newspaper that espoused Mussolini and blamed the Jews for the turmoil in Europe; and the local headquarters of Father Coughlin, the priest whose popular radio program for years promoted Hitler, fascism and anti-Semitism, and damned FDR and the New Deal.

Although there were a few Jewish families in the area, we each pretty much kept to ourselves, trying not to call attention to our existence, but just wanting to be left alone in individual peace. There was condescending participation in sports on the nearby playgrounds and recreation parks, and grudging admittance to the street games like roller hockey or stickball or ringalevio or pitching pennies around the stoops of the rows of small brown brick houses that lined the streets. When any Jewish kids did mix in, accepted for the moment, their names automatically became "Jew-boy" or "Christ-killer" and before a day's play was over they likely as not would be picked on or challenged to a fight by one or more of the kids they were playing with. Many of the kids in the neighborhood went to the church school, and when they talked about what they learned there, it often seemed to be about how the Jews killed Christ and how Hitler was doing what should have been done a long time ago. I didn't know whether the teaching nuns were responsible for that or *The Tablet* or Father Coughlin's radio shows or the kid's parents. Maybe it was all of them put together?

When I didn't want to face the harsh realities of my neighborhood, I escaped by reading adventure books and by spending as many of my hard-saved or parent-offered dimes on tickets to the movies, which cost only ten cents for kids during the 1930s. In the darkness of the movie theater I could pretend to be one of the good guys on the screen, triumphing over the bad guys. Even after the movie was over I would hold on to the aura of whatever actor played the good guy in the film I had just seen, and sometimes when I didn't want to deal with a difficult situation I imagined I was one of my movie heroes and tried to figure out what he would do in that circumstance.

Anyway, I didn't like to see anybody, especially an underdog, picked on, and more than once got a bloodied nose for it. It wasn't for religious reasons. My parents weren't religious. I did not attend the synagogue on Fourth Avenue, about a mile from where I lived. Some non-Jewish kids in the neighborhood and their parents would sometimes ask me to join them at their religious services. I looked on it as a social occasion. Maybe their purpose was what they considered an altruistic attempt to save my soul? At one time or another I attended Catholic, Lutheran, Baptist, Greek Orthodox, Methodist, as well as Jewish services. To tell the truth, I was never convinced by any of them. They all seemed to ignore the reality of life going on about them—like the war in Ethiopia, the pogroms against the Jews in Germany and the people starving right in front of them on the streets in Brooklyn—and appeared to spend their time praying for some amorphous being to do something about it rather than taking the responsibility upon themselves to solve the problems. I vividly remember coming home from one of those services with a classmate and his parents one evening when a man walked up to one of the steel stanchions holding up the Third Avenue elevated tracks and began punching the girder, blood spraying from his knuckles and hands onto his face and clothes and the sidewalk. He saw us and stopped a moment. "I'm dying," he yelled. "My wife and kids, they're dying. We ain't got no food. I can't get no job." He turned back to the pillar and began pounding it again in frustration, exhaling a plaintive "sonuvabitch" every time his fist crashed into it.

I looked up at my friend's parents. "Can't we help him? Can't we do anything?"

"God will take care of him," was the answer. "These are hard times and we must trust in God." And then, "He's probably just a drunk, anyway."

Well, no god had taken care of that man or the six million Jews and the forty-five million others of all religions who were killed during World War II, and I had no expectation that a god—whatever he or she or it might be—was going to take care of the survivors at St. Ottilien.

～　　　　☞　　　　～

After Dr. Grinberg finished his liberation concert speech, the people remained where they were for a long while, then gradually began to walk toward the buildings, silently and alone. Some moved painfully, leaning on others. Some were carried on makeshift stretchers. A few stayed, sitting or lying by themselves, staring at the sky. Were they thinking about the past? About the future? Or trying not to think at all? A few talked quietly. The power of the music, the drama of Dr. Grinberg's odyssey, had settled into a sadness that encompassed everything, a heaviness that seemed to reduce life to a plodding moment-by-moment existence. I found myself walking very slowly and carefully so as not to disturb the feeling that surrounded me. I waited until most of the crowd, including a number of men in U.S. Army uniforms and some well-dressed civilians, had gone, then sought out Dr. Grinberg.

His confident manner was reinforced by his clear, straightforward tone and excellent command of the English language.

I introduced myself and told him that I wanted to help. He led the way to his office, a corner room in one of the buildings with an outside entrance of its own. A desk and chair against the wall opposite the door, an old couch and another chair made up the main part of the room, and to the right, partially hidden by a curtain hanging on a rod across the ceiling, was a small area with a bed, a night table and a dresser.

"I edit an army newspaper," I told him, "I'm going to do a story on the hospital here. I'll send it to the United States. I'm sure once the people there know what is happening, you'll get the help you need." I sounded Pollyanna-ish, even to myself.

"We appreciate any help. We need it to survive. Do you really believe you can let the world know about us? And if they know about us, will they pay attention?" Was he asking because I was an American who came from the real world of the living and might somehow know the answers, or were his questions purely rhetorical? "The world forgot about us for the past ten years. Why would they care about us now?" The words were cynical, but his tone was gentle.

"Many of the people in the United States didn't know," I said defensively.

"Didn't know?"

"Well, didn't believe."

I sat on the couch, he sat in the chair by the desk, facing me.

"Didn't believe there were death camps?" He looked at me patiently, as a teacher with a pupil who hasn't taken time to think before answering. "Have you been to Dachau?"

"Yes. I've seen it."

"You've seen the railroad station? Where people arrived from all over Europe, thousands every month, to be taken to the camp?"

"Yes."

"You've seen the furnaces? Where until only a few weeks ago hundreds of people were going up in smoke every day."

I nodded.

"Have you talked to the people in the city of Dachau? Have you asked any of them if they knew about the camp there?"

"I've talked to some," I answered. "Very few say they knew about it. And no one admits knowing what went on there."

"Have you found one German who admits knowing what went on in any of the camps?"

"None," I admitted.

"You don't think that is strange?"

"Of course. They had to know." I felt anger now. He had transferred some of his into me. "Everybody in Germany had to know what was going on," I blurted. "There's no way they couldn't have known unless they were deaf and blind and had no sense of smell."

"And nobody in America wondered what happened to the Jews and the others who disappeared from their homes? The Jews in America didn't wonder what happened to relatives they no longer heard from? The newspapers in America didn't print anything about what was happening here?"

"You're right, Dr. Grinberg," I said. "We knew when we wanted to know. But I guess, like everyone else, we wanted to pretend we didn't know so we wouldn't have to do anything about it. That way, we didn't feel guilty."

"And now you believe it will change?"

"I think it is different now. The war is over. They can send organizations to help. They don't have to depend on politics to tell them what they can or can't do."

"In your great country of America, in free democratic America, people just wait on politics to tell them if they can be human beings or not?"

I thought for a moment. Though I knew he was right, I felt uncomfortable being part of a mind game that seemed intent on bashing my country. "I think that's so in all countries," I said. "People become frightened. They think that by joining the majority they can escape being a minority."

"Ah," Dr. Grinberg smiled. "Do you really believe that the people of America, including the Jews, will stop going along with the majority of the world and do something now for the surviving Jews of Europe?"

"I really do," I said. I wasn't that sure, but if I didn't think it and say it, then the alternative was to believe that there was no hope for the future. "Things are better than they were. We did win the war. You are free from the camps. You have a place to live. You did have a liberation concert today."

"Did you see joy today? Did you see normal people? It was a marking, a moment, a passing. We have no food, no clothing, no medicine. How long can we survive on music? Or on words? We cannot even, as other people do, live on memories. Memories make it worse. So we hold a liberation concert and maybe for a few days it will psychologically help people resist hunger a little better. But we have little hope. We have already been out in the postwar world, not only the world of the Germans, but the world of the Americans. Shall I tell you what we went through getting here?"

He told me how the survivors at St. Ottilien were liberated.

At the end of April 1945, while people in cities large and small throughout most of the Western world celebrated the anticipated end of World War II in Europe, and while people in Germany and many other countries in eastern and western Europe gathered in small, fearful, clandestine groups to mourn in shocked disbelief the reported death of Adolf Hitler, seven hundred ragged, diseased, wounded, malnourished, skeletal beings wearing only the gray-and-white striped uniforms of the concentration camps staggered with automaton steps from the railroad depot of Dachau onto the roads of Germany.

Herding them together like a benevolent shepherd trying to keep intact a disoriented, straying flock was Zalman Grinberg. He was a plain-looking man, not at all like the Hollywood version of either a resistance leader or a modern Moses. His mien, however, belying his appearance both by nature and necessity, was one of utmost self-confidence.

Dr. Grinberg was one of the few physicians to survive the concentration camps. Originally from Lithuania, he had suffered the same anguish as the other Jews of Europe, from the torment of the ghettos to the death and dying of the camps. He had managed to stay together with his wife and 13-year-old son until one year earlier, when upon their arrival at the train depot at Tiegenhof as part of a shipment of Jews ostensibly going from Kovno to the concentration camp at Stutthof, his wife and son were sent off in one direction, whether to the gas chambers or to a slave labor camp he didn't know, and he was led away in another, to Dachau.

In April of 1945 the prisoners in Dachau knew the war was going badly for the Germans because there were fewer and fewer soldiers guarding them. One day they were told that they were being repatriated by the International Red Cross to Switzerland. However, on April 14 Heinrich Himmler had issued orders that no concentration camp prisoners should be allowed to fall into Allied hands. Because Eisenhower refused to issue orders that the camps be liberated, the camp inmates had not yet been repatriated and now were to be annihilated.

Some fifteen hundred prisoners from the concentration camps at Dachau and Buchenwald were put into trucks and driven to an assembly point at a railhead not far from the Dachau camp, where they awaited the arrival of boxcars to take them to their destination. When they saw that SS troops had been assigned to guard them and they were forced to stand several hours without rest, food or water, they knew they had been tricked again, that they were not being repatriated by the Red Cross. In reality, they were being evacuated to the Tyrol, to be exterminated there. They realized that this would be their final journey and that they and all the others still in the camps would be executed before the Allies would rescue them. A few, clinging to survival by refusing to accept the consistency of Nazi behavior, hoped that maybe they would only be held as hostages.

It was almost evening when these fifteen hundred abruptly got their chance for freedom.

The railroad depot was also at that time an ammunition collection point and was piled high with boxes and crates of ammunition and powder. Suddenly a flight of American planes swooped down, bombing and strafing. In the confusion the prisoners ran, some caught by the bombs and bullets, others gunned down by the Germans. But some escaped into a nearby area of trees and bushes. As the air attack continued, the German soldiers and civilians took whatever trucks and cars there were and fled, seeking shelter and anonymity from both the planes and the approaching American Army. As the bombing and strafing went on, the prisoners who had run into the wooded area were soon joined by a number of German soldiers who had not been able to flee. The prisoners felt an elation they had not known for years, seeing the Germans facing the same threat of death as they, with the wooded area as well as the railhead becoming a target for the American planes. In the morning, when they emerged from their hiding places, fewer than eight hundred of the prisoners remained alive. The survivors found themselves alone in the unearthly quiet of the railroad square. Many were bleeding from wounds received in the bombing. Many lay dead, an ending to their lives they would have considered merciful only a few days before. But now, if they had been alive to consider it, their deaths were horribly ironic. Those who had survived were barely more mobile, disease and starvation inherited from years in the camps continuing to do what the bombs and bullets had not.

They looked around at the silent streets, virtually empty except for themselves. They looked at each other and were afraid to risk disappointment by openly acknowledging what seemed to be: They were free. Inexplicably, they were free.

Had they the strength and the psychological will, they would have danced with joy, opened their arms wide to the physical freshness of freedom. A few thought they would like to do so, but instead they stood, sat or lay where they were, looking only at the sky, trying to comprehend what it meant to be free, then lowering their gaze from the openness of the sky to the confinement of the buildings surrounding them, knowing that it couldn't be what it seemed and that at any moment the Germans surely would be back and put them once again behind the gates of Dachau or Buchenwald or shoot them right where they were. After several hours of remaining close together, barely moving, the group protectiveness more comforting than real in the event the Germans did return, they began to believe that perhaps they really might be free, after all. A few tentatively began to wander to the square, to cautiously peer around the corner of a building or walk several paces into another street, as if to assure themselves that there was a continuing, tangible world out there.

As the day lengthened and dusk approached, more and more

survivors, those who could walk, began to wander off to look for food and shelter. Dr. Grinberg knew that an individual or even a small group would have difficulty surviving, not only because of the starvation and disease that afflicted them, but because those away from the main body would more likely to be set upon and shot or beaten to death by Germans who might see them. Although pretenses of being anti-Nazi would later be the key to the Germans' salvation when confronted by their American conquerors, Dr. Grinberg knew that the German attitudes and actions of the past fifteen years would not suddenly change just because they had been beaten in a war that now was almost at an end.

Dr. Grinberg gathered together the most able-bodied people he could find and established cadres to round up as many of the survivors as possible. For several days they stayed in the area, looked for food in shops and homes that had been abandoned by the fleeing population and searched for more survivors.

Eight hundred survivors of Dachau and Buchenwald, a wandering band, staying close together, carrying on makeshift wagons and carriages those who could not walk, sleeping huddled together at night, sharing whatever scraps of food could be foraged and the occasional edible plants growing in fields alongside the road, moving silently and slowly toward the west, the direction from which the Americans were coming. Every day more died. Dr. Grinberg hoped to keep alive as many as possible until they encountered the Americans, who he was certain would give them the help they needed. Their priority was in finding food.

Every day, in every town they came to, Dr. Grinberg went to the Bürgermeister and begged for food. Even though the Germans knew the war was ending, they gave nothing. The survivors were fortunate that only old men, young boys and women remained in the towns or they would have been recaptured and probably shot on the spot. There were some German soldiers about, but they were deserters who were too busy looking out for themselves. Even so, almost every place the survivors went, they were spat upon, beaten, stoned and ordered out of town before they could even stop and rest. The Germans' attitude clearly had not changed, and if they could starve these survivors to death to help complete Hitler's "final solution," so much the better. Dr. Grinberg was refused food from every quarter.

In the first week of May 1945, they reached the town of Buchloe, near Landsberg. Dr. Grinberg vainly pleaded for help, but as soon as the Bürgermeister realized that Dr. Grinberg was the leader of a group of Jews, he had two of his assistants grab Dr. Grinberg by the arms and carry him to the doorway of the office, about to throw him out. Suddenly, a commotion coming from the street stopped them. The Bürgermeister ran to the window to find out the cause of the excitement. The people were screaming that the Americans were coming, that they were less than an hour away.

As Dr. Grinberg later told me, "until that moment, everywhere I had gone, I was addressed as '*Schweinhund, Verfluchte Jud*, dirty Jew.' Now, with the Americans near, the Bürgermeister had his men release my arms and he quietly turned to me. 'Won't you have a seat, my honored sir, and let us see how we can help your poor people.'"

"That," Dr. Grinberg later recalled with a smile of satisfaction that contradicted his usual lack of self-indulgence, "was the moment of my liberation."

If the survivors thought that the Americans would provide them with the food, medicine, clothing and shelter they needed, they were mistaken. In the days that followed, Dr. Grinberg and his band of survivors were to find a new road of torture, pain and frustration. True, they now were really free. But they had sacrificed everything, had taken more punishment than any other people had ever known. Now they were martyrs, martyrs returning from the grave. They had expected to be treated as such, that everything possible would be done for them to try to help them get past what they had endured and suffered, to help them continue to live. Yet, within three weeks hundreds more of this group would be dead from the lack of food and medicine.

Dr. Grinberg continued to visit the heads of the various towns they came to, but this time, instead of encountering Bürgermeisters, he found American Army officers. If he expected to find a different attitude as well, he was wrong. The answers were the same as they had been before, only in more polite terms. One of the officers he visited was a captain in Landsberg, who said that he would like to help, but that he was unable to because there were no supplies available. A Captain Rhein, who later became commanding officer of the U.S. Military Government in Landsberg, was sympathetic and promised to help, but as it turned out, Dr. Grinberg told me, didn't. Most of the officers Dr. Grinberg went to displayed an outward sympathy, but when it came to actually providing assistance, sympathy seemed to be all that they could muster. Possibly it was because of old attitudes, reflecting the United States position before and during the war of refusing help to the Jews of Europe. Possibly, with the influence of the German people the offic-

ers were meeting, especially educated German women who became their interpreters, secretaries and in many cases, their mistresses, it was because some were developing new attitudes.

Each company commander and almost every American soldier Dr. Grinberg and his group met said they wanted to help, but
except for a few pounds of rice or potatoes smuggled from an army
kitchen, some loaves of bread passed out the back door of a mess
hall, some rations from individual soldiers, there was no help. None
of the army units they met seemed to be able to find, in Dr.
Grinberg's words, "enough extra supplies" to give to them.

"American goods were plentiful," Dr. Grinberg later recalled,
"but they were going to the black market. Somehow, none of the
American officers or commanders could find any for us. Most of them
gave us a lot of sympathy. But none of them gave us any help."

Unless they could get food and locate a shelter that could be
converted into a hospital, many more survivors would soon die.
Within Dr. Grinberg's group were five more physicians. Like him,
they had false occupations listed on their papers when they entered the concentration camps, and unlike other professionals who
were among the first to be killed, they survived. If Dr. Grinberg
could find quarters, food and medicine to nurse the doctors back to
health, they in turn might be able to save many of the others.

In slow measured steps, going no more than a couple of miles
a day, stopping frequently to rest, taking time for the able-bodied
to search for food, comforting the sick and burying the dead, by
the end of another week they had come to the church and monas-
tery village of St. Ottilien, about eighteen miles west of Landsberg.
St. Ottilien was old, wealthy and large, a core of stone buildings

surrounding the bountiful church, these buildings in turn surrounded by a number of wooden structures. Apart from the main church area, all of it ostensibly was being used as a hospital for German officers and soldiers. A group of eight outbuildings, comprising the hospital area, was set apart from the main enclave by a large greensward. Four buildings seemed to be unoccupied or barely in use. Although they were not ideal for a hospital, they would make considerably better quarters than any of the survivors had had for a number of years.

Dr. Grinberg knew that it would be pointless for him to attempt to obtain any space by himself. The German commandant might not throw him out, with American troops nearby, but he certainly would not relinquish any space to concentration camp survivors even though, as Dr. Grinberg was prepared to show, some members of his group were not Jewish. Dr. Grinberg went to the military headquarters of Landsberg again, and then to Buchloe, but in both places was refused authorization to appropriate any of the buildings at St. Ottilien. It looked like the end of the road for this band of survivors. They might well die where they were, in the thick-grassed field across from a side gate of St. Ottilien.

But Dr. Grinberg had a scheme.

If he could find one American officer, he thought, who would be willing to cooperate, he just might pull it off. He found the officer in the person of Captain Otto B. Raymond, in an infantry regiment a few miles away. Learning of the plight of this group of survivors, Captain Raymond, who was from St. Louis, devoted his energies to helping them.

"I'm not a Jew," Dr. Grinberg later told me Captain Raymond

had said to him, "but it only matters that one is a human being to hate what the Nazis have done."

Captain Raymond agreed to go along with Dr. Grinberg's plan, in which Dr. Grinberg would pose as a representative of the International Red Cross, and got him appropriate civilian clothes and a false identification card. Together they went to the commandant of the German hospital at St. Ottilien, where Captain Raymond ordered him to relinquish space for Dr. Grinberg and the by-then four hundred and twenty remaining survivors. The commandant refused on the grounds that the German soldiers there were too sick to be moved. Dr. Grinberg and Captain Raymond found that most of the Germans seemed to be in good health and appeared to be using St. Ottilien principally as a hideaway, so as not to be interned by the American forces. With Captain Raymond supporting him, Dr. Grinberg, in his guise of an International Red Cross official, threatened dire consequences if the commandant didn't yield at least four of the outbuildings. He warned that the Red Cross would investigate the use being made of the entire complex, with the threat that it might be expropriated in its entirety. The German commandant yielded.

It was two weeks after V-E Day that the surviving four hundred and twenty moved into what was to become the first and only hospital in the U.S.-occupied zone of Germany for survivors of the Holocaust.

"You see," he said to me as he finished this account, "we have had to do everything for ourselves. Do you wonder why I question whether we will get any help from the outside?"

"I want to try," I said, "and I'm sure there are others who want to try. We've got to at least do that."

He got up and sat on the couch, next to me. He put his hand on my arm, then on my shoulder. "You care about human life. You care about us. You are optimistic. That is good. But you should also be realistic. Why should you become disappointed and cynical as we are? Be prepared for that."

"We'll get what you need," I said. "Some way. What is most critical?"

"Food. Medicine. There are many sick and injured we could still save. And every day, from all over Germany, dozens more arrive at St. Ottilien. Every day, as some die, some get well enough to leave, to return to their homelands to look for some trace of their families. There are more than enough waiting to take their places. Warm clothing and blankets are not yet urgent, with summer coming. But in the fall and winter there will be many more dead unless we have them."

He was in deep thought for a moment. Maybe it was the sorrow of contemplation of the future. Suddenly he looked up brightly. "Would you like to see what we have done with our little hospital here? Would you like to meet some of the people?"

I nodded.

"Come." He motioned for me to follow him and led me from his office to the next building. There were two floors, both with large open rooms filled with cots, with mattresses on the floor, with chairs placed next to each other, with flat boards sitting on wooden or stone supports, all serving as beds. On every one lay a person wearing the too-familiar striped pajama uniform. Dr. Grinberg took me to a corner of the room where five beds were set apart from the others. A man was sitting on the edge of one; the men lying in the others had the sagging, sickly look of the seriously ill. "These are all doctors in these beds," Dr. Grinberg said. "We destroyed our identifications and had papers with false occupations. They didn't know we were doctors or they would have killed us. The Germans killed all the elite first. The professions. The doctors, the teachers, the artists, the scientists. And the children. They wanted to make sure the Jews were entirely destroyed. If anyone was to survive, it would be the dregs. Or so they thought. We are among the few Jewish doctors who may have survived the camps. We are the only ones in this part of Germany. But so far I alone have been able to work." He introduced me to the man sitting on the edge of the cot.

"In a short time Dr. Katz should be well enough to work, too," Dr. Grinberg said. "This will make a big difference. Our priority is to get the doctors healthy as soon as possible. Then we will have a better chance of saving some of the others."

I met several of the other patients in the hospital. One of the survivors I met stays in my memory to this day. He was a little boy, perhaps 10 years old. While he reacted like a child to the candy and gum I would bring him every time I visited St. Ottilien, he also had an arrogance and swagger that one associates with defiance or bravado in males twice his age. The first time I saw him he was wearing a short-sleeved white shirt and short leather pants, probably liberated from an abandoned German house as he and the others made their way to St. Ottilien. He had a round face, and even when he wasn't talking his mouth seemed to hang open, in anticipation of saying something, or as some people do when they listen intently, as if on guard against what he might hear. I was not surprised to see the fuzzy blue numbers of the concentration camp tattoo stand out on his left forearm. But it disturbed me to see it on a child, even though I had by then seen it on many adults. When I first saw survivors with the tattoos I would stare at them, as if my disbelief would somehow make the numbers disappear. I quickly got used to them and stopped staring. Still, it felt different to see it on a small child.

The boy was called Tito. It was not his real name and I don't think I ever learned what his real name was. Tito was proud of his nickname and didn't hesitate to tell anyone willing to listen that he got it because he had fought with the partisans in Yugoslavia under Marshal Tito. Many little children six, eight, 10 years old, alone in the world and dependent only on themselves, fought to survive any way they could during the war. They had no other choice. Tito said his parents had fought with a partisan group in Yugoslavia and had been killed and the partisans had taken care of him until he was captured by the Germans just before the war ended and sent to an extermination camp. There weren't many children who survived. Tito played an important role in the months ahead helping American soldiers smuggle food into St. Ottilien.

At one point Dr. Grinberg asked me if I wanted to see some of the more seriously ill. I said yes and he took me to the second floor. He pointed to the door in front of us. "Maybe you don't want to go in?" he asked me. His question was more pertinent to my sensibility than to my curiosity. He pushed it partially open. No one was standing or even sitting. People lay on their cots as if they were in a morgue. I looked quickly along the rows and rows of bodies. Some of them twitched. Some lay still, with no movement at all. A low, continuing sound of moaning filled the room, echoing in waves from one side to the other. Every few seconds there would be heavy coughing. Some of it sounded like retching.

"There are over a hundred people in here," Dr. Grinberg said. "Dozens will soon be dead. And dozens more will come to take their places. Right now there is very little we can do to help any of them." He closed the door.

We walked slowly back to his office, not talking. I felt nauseous, like I was about to faint, and I breathed deep gulps of air and dug my nails into my palms to take my mind off the sweaty, tight feeling in my head and eyes.

We sat down where we had been before, me on the couch, Dr. Grinberg at his desk. He gave me a chance to collect myself.

"You know," I said, "when we talked before and I said that I would do what I could to help, I meant it. But now that you have shown me a little bit of what it's like here, I mean it even more. I'd like to bring some of the other fellows on the base here. The more help, the better."

"We will be grateful," Dr. Grinberg said.

"Almost all of us in America, our parents or grandparents or great-grandparents came from Europe," I said, "and had they not come we might be here at St. Ottilien or killed in some concentration camp."

Dr. Grinberg was silent, then looked away and stared at the wall on the other side of the room. I sensed what he might be thinking. "Have you heard anything about your family?" I asked. "Do you know whether they are still alive?"

He continued to stare, not answering

"I'm sorry," I apologized. "I shouldn't have asked."

"No, no. It is all right. I appreciate you caring." He got up, walked across the room, then to the door and stood as he talked. "As soon as we were free we sent out the healthiest men with the names and addresses of all of the relatives of the people who had survived the railroad depot in Dachau. They walked, rode, somehow got back to each of the towns where the people here had lived, to see if anyone had come back or had sent messages where they were, and to leave messages for anyone who might return. A few days ago the man we had sent to Lithuania found us here. No one had any word of my wife or son. Except one person who heard they had been killed." He took a handkerchief from his pocket, opened it completely and held it over his entire face, then crumpled it up against his eyes. "So what can I do but cry? It was a hope."

I walked over to him and put my hand on his shoulder as if I were an old friend, not an accidental acquaintance, a youngster half his age. He reached up and patted my hand.

"By now I should have learned not to cry," he said. "But even when you think you have no more life, some tears remain. And maybe even some laughter. I hope you never have to live through what we have lived through."

I went to my jeep and started back to Kaufbeuren. I knew I was much more involved in St. Ottilien than just being a reporter doing a story for the *2nd Wing Eagle*. I didn't realize then how attending the liberation concert would change my life and, as it turned out, the lives of many others.

# Chapter 4 ～

## U.S. POLICY AND PRACTICE

The policies and practices of the U.S. occupation forces didn't bode well for the survivors at St. Ottilien or at many of the other refugee centers that began to spring up in the occupied zones of Germany and Austria. Ironically, in many instances former concentration camps and detention centers were put into use to accommodate thousands of these camps' former inmates who had no other place to go.

While such quarters were appropriated by the U.S. forces and in most cases turned over to the survivors, rarely were any provisions also provided—neither food, clothing nor medicine. The sight of survivors walking around in the striped-pajama uniforms, and in the same or similar concentration camps where they had been imprisoned, was both galling and frightening.

During the first few weeks following the end of the war, the U.S. Military Government had not yet begun full operation. The officers in charge of individual cities and towns were mostly the commanders of the military units that had taken those areas and remained in it, or whose outfits had been brought in after the first units had moved on. Most had seen war up close and would brook no coddling of the recent enemy. The Supreme Headquarters' non-fraternization order was strongly enforced, and any GI who wandered off base, either on official business or unofficially to go to a whorehouse or the home of a German mistress, was wise to carry a gun. For weeks after the war was over U.S. soldiers were found dead in woods and streams and back alleys, usually beaten to death or with their throats slashed, often lured there by German women. Several of the men at our Kaufbeuren air base died that way. Some of us called those first weeks National Lorelei Month.

The Germans had not yet learned how easily they could fool the Americans into thinking they had all been anti-Nazis. At first, when the war ended, the Germans were frightened. They expected the Americans to act the same way their own troops had acted when taking over another country. They were surprised that there weren't mass reprisals. Drawing on their own experiences as conquerors, they assumed that the Americans would be angered at the atrocities they, the Germans, had committed, and they expected immediate, full and hard retribution. They thought they had nothing to lose. They cursed the Jews as the cause of their defeat. They sneered at the late President Franklin D. Roosevelt. They talked about the glory of Nazism. They praised Hitler and refused to believe that the leader who had promised them a Thousand Year Reich had actually killed himself in a bunker in Berlin. Nazism had been their life, their staff and their glory for over a dozen years. This did not change because someone said that May 8 was V-E Day.

The killing of GIs stopped, except for sporadic forays by a hard-core youth group know as "werewolves"—similar to the skinheads, the neo-Nazis of Germany in the 1990s. The Germans learned quickly that they could defeat the American occupation aims more easily by guile, wile and smile than by confrontation.

It wasn't all that difficult.

Following the end of hostilities, the American soldiers were weary. A man weary of war does not stop to think of political or societal ethics or even a quarter million dead buddies when he finds he no longer needs to be tired and dejected. As with all conquering armies, the Americans found it was time to make up for the hell they gone through. After the first few weeks of assessing the situation, the Germans gave them the opportunity.

Within a month after the end of the war most of the GIs seemed to love Germany. The German people were so polite. They outdid each other to serve the American soldiers. They ran, they fetched, they bowed, they cringed, they brought beer and cheese and cameras and binoculars and their daughters and themselves. They offered soft beds and fresh sheets and fine furniture and clean houses and plumbing that worked better than any the soldiers had seen in France or Belgium or Holland. The GIs were tired of war and felt it was time they were treated with the deference and the material satisfactions that they, as conquerors, believed they were entitled to.

This had not been so in the Allied countries. There we were treated not as conquerors, but as equals. There we had to buy what we wanted. In Germany we only had to take, whether it was a woman, a camera or a bottle of schnapps. If we felt like it, we could leave a pack of cigarettes or a chocolate bar or some sugar to ease our conscience. Not that we had to take very often. Most of the time it was freely offered. Perhaps that's because the Germans knew that cigarettes and candy and food were always forthcoming in exchange.

Cigarettes quickly became the most prized and valuable commodity in Germany. A week's Post Exchange ration of a carton of cigarettes could bring the equivalent of a month's military salary on the black market. A pack of cigarettes could buy a couple bottles of schnapps or a night in bed with a blond-haired, blue-eyed Fraulein.

The American soldiers—or at least most of them, it seemed—gloried in it. Teenagers, young men in their 20s, older men in their 30s had had no such power or opportunity back in the States. They knew they would not be likely to have it again once they returned home, and they vied with each other to take fullest advantage of it.

They liked it so much that soon many were wondering how it was that these fine, cooperative, warm and friendly people could have been their enemy. The GI began to think that these Germans weren't such bad people, after all. The *Why We Fight* series, prepared by Hollywood producer Frank Capra and shown to all U.S. troops before they were shipped overseas, must have been just propaganda! The Germans really weren't to blame for what happened. They were led; they were forced to follow. Concentration camps, atrocities at Lidice, Warsaw, Lublin? The people didn't know about that. Certainly not these "good" Germans who had become the GIs' friends. Ask almost any American soldier who served in the U.S. occupation in Germany after World War II, and he or she will tell you that they never came across an admitted Nazi.

The Germans seemed so much like Americans. The Fraulein was like the girl next door. Her family was like the friendly, hospitable neighbors we knew back home.

"Shee-ee-t, these are good people, why it's just like bein' back home, visitin' the girlfriend, eatin' dinner with the people next door. And they got their places fixed up just like we got, not that old broken-down crap like the Limeys and the Frogs got."

If it occurred to the GI that many of the furnishings in German homes had been stolen from other countries, if there was a thought that the plumbing worked and the unbombed houses were in good repair because the Germans had kept their economy up at the expense of the economies of the countries they had ravaged, these thoughts disappeared when the GI was in a German home surrounded by people treating him like he was a close friend or relative. Although the American soldier remembered that the Germans had been the enemy and the French, the Belgians, the English and the Dutch our allies, the Germans somehow made him feel as if he were closer to them and shared more with them than with the others, and that maybe, just maybe, the war itself may have been a mistake.

Most of the GIs didn't think it was strange that they never met a German who had been a Nazi. Most of the Germans told how they had been forced into the war against their will. None, of course, had known anything about the concentration camps. The alleged atrocities of the Third Reich had come as a complete surprise when they heard about them after the war, they all insisted. Some of the Americans were confused. Since none of the Germans they met had any knowledge of the evil things Hitler supposedly had been doing, could all the allegations about atrocities and concentration camps be, as their German friends hinted, communist propaganda, deliberately distorting what had happened in order to turn the United States against Germany, its best future ally and the staunchest enemy of the communist menace in Europe?

"Hell, these people admit they were wrong to fight us. They didn't want to, they just wanted to get the Rooskis. They shouldn't be blamed because some of their leaders, the war criminals, misled them. The damned Limeys, with their accents, think they're so superior and the damned Frogs won't speak English when you're around, so you know they're conniving against you, so in a way you can't blame the Germans for going to war against them."

When an American soldier was lying in bed with one or more of the women or girls of the family and bloated with food and drink and sex, it wasn't too difficult for his bed partner to get him to wonder how it might have been if Germany and America had been allies.

Although the non-fraternization rule ostensibly prevented American soldiers from having personal relationships with German civilians, few GIs could resist the open welcome and smiling services that satisfied virtually their every need. The influence on officers and men alike of these German efforts to win the peace may have been the reason for the lack of almost any attempts at reeducation by the occupying military government. Or perhaps it was the lack of a strong reeducation program that encouraged the Germans to try to win over the occupying forces to their way of thinking? If there were any Madison Avenue experts in the American MG, they apparently were not given much opportunity to practice their trade. The principal American information efforts were signs posted on buildings showing drawings of concentration camp horrors, with the words *"Deine Schulde"*—Your Fault. Apparently believing the Germans' protestations that they had no idea what

had been going on during the dozen years they had supported the
Nazi regime, the military government assumed that the signs were
sufficient to bring about instant humanitarian attitudes. Apparently,
it did not seem to occur to anyone in a policy-making position that
the Germans may have known all along what was going on and that
what was shown on the posters was not interpreted by the Germans as a fault but a depiction of the mission and duty they had
dedicated themselves to over the years. The American efforts were
laughed at by the Germans, who paid no more attention to the
posters than they had to the same information and knowledge about
the extermination camps during the previous decade.

If the Germans expected the Americans to attempt to destroy their beliefs in Nazism or to reeducate them to democratic
ideals, they were wrong. There were no public speeches, no classroom lectures, no door-to-door "missionaries." For many months
the schools were closed, and when they reopened in the fall of
1945 the military government seemed oblivious to what was going
on in the classrooms. German children continued to learn out of
many of the same books they had used before and with almost all
of the same teachers who had taught them, under the Third Reich,
to be good Hitler *Jugend*. The American authorities appeared to
take no interest in their education or reeducation. Little, if any,
attempt appeared to be made to teach either the adults or the youth
that what Germany had done was wrong, and that a democratic
type of government, a non-fascist government, should emerge in
the postwar world.

Many of the Nazi officials remained in their jobs. "So what
if this guy was mayor under Hitler. We need experienced admin-

istrators to keep these towns running. He can't do anything bad while we keep an eye on him." Many Nazi Bürgermeisters who ran local governments under Hitler continued to run them under the Americans.

Every MG officer had an interpreter. This was usually a highly educated, highly attractive, relatively young German woman. Before he died—"supposedly" died, many GIs said—Hitler reportedly made a speech in which he told the German women that if the German soldiers did not win the war, that they, the women, must win the peace. Considering everything else that they had done for the Führer and the Fatherland, this was little enough to be asked and little enough to do. And they did.

Many of the interpreters had studied abroad, most in England, some in America. Many came from upper middle class and upper class families. Some had been wealthy. Some still were. Most were able to dress well and had makeup that most other women in Germany could not get. Whether they were as attractive in bed depended on the expectations of their bedmates, but that was one of their principal dedications and duties. What red-blooded young American, exposed to the sophistication of old Europe for the first time, given a feeling of official power along with the glory of serving his country, could not be flattered, satisfied, overwhelmed, taken in and, finally, controlled by a pretty Fraulein who interpreted for him, looked good for him, ran the office for him, attended to liaison duties for him and fucked for him?

Many displaced persons, especially Jews, knowing no English, had gone to American MG offices and been turned away without help, not knowing till long afterward, if ever, that the interpreter had deliberately translated incorrectly and that the American officer in charge had never really learned who they were or what they wanted. Some officers knew or at least suspected, but insecure in their knowledge of politics and history, accepted what their German mistresses told them, especially when told in the comfort of their own beds. It wasn't their fault, some began to think, if the U.S. government had neglected to tell them the truth that the Jews really were the cause of the war and that it was in our country's best interests to continue the final solution.

Some of the MG heads, young officers who were put in charge of individual cities and towns, not only reflected but reinforced these attitudes.

Typical was the experience of two young Polish Jewish sisters who survived the war by working as slave laborers under false papers that listed them as non-Jews, and now found themselves, at the ages of 16 and 17, in Kaufbeuren.

I first met Adele when Eli Isaacson, one of the soldiers on the base, brought her to my office. She had come to the personnel office looking for a job. Whoever was on duty that day didn't speak any German, but Eli spoke the language extremely well and was assigned to take care of her. He brought her to me to see if I could help.

She appeared at the door like a fearful mouse, tentatively looking in, wondering whether she could advance another inch without being swatted or crushed. I sensed her more than I saw her. She was short, wearing a flabby, no-color dress, brownish hair wisping on top of a face of two large frightened eyes. She appeared to be about 15, or maybe 20, maybe even 30. She was like a line drawing of a person, an amorphous being.

*"Ich such arbeit."*

I could barely hear her. She said each word as if she were waiting for permission to speak the next one. The softness and lowness and hesitancy came out like a human squeak.

While my two years of high school German were barely adequate, it was more than most GIs knew, and sometimes I even acted as an unofficial interpreter. I was able to speak with Adele directly.

She obviously was not German. She had neither the fawning manner that flattered some American soldiers nor the arrogance that other American soldiers mistook for dignity and strength. I knew she was a displaced person. She stood silently. She had learned that you don't speak without first being spoken to. One might say the wrong thing and get into serious trouble. That was a cardinal principle of survival that most of us learned, whether under the Nazis, in the army or in a classroom.

"What kind of job are you looking for?" I asked in German.

"Any kind of job."

The base was besieged daily by D.P.s and Germans looking for jobs. The Second Wing had already hired about as many as it could for the menial tasks that otherwise would be done by GIs: kitchen work, cleaning buildings and toilets, sweeping the walkways, repairing streets, emptying wastebaskets and just running for coffee. With few jobs still available, she ordinarily would have been turned away at the gate. I was glad she had reached me. I felt a strange interdependency with her, as if she were a relative I hadn't known existed but who I now felt an obligation to care of.

I wanted to know who she was, but the only thing I learned

was from her identification papers, which described her as a 16-year-old Catholic from Poland. I knew the mess sergeant and asked Adele—her papers listed her name as Lydia—if she would be interested in a job in the kitchen. Her answer was a wordless, hesitant nod. Eli and I took her to the mess hall. "Cookie" gave her a job.

A few days later, as I passed through the chow line, she was standing there, dishing out food. Over the next few weeks I got an extra large helping of whatever she was serving, at breakfast, lunch and dinner. I always said a few words as I passed, usually asking her if the job was all right. At first I got nods, after a while a few mumbled words of acknowledgment, later an occasional smile. Then one day she spoke hurriedly as I passed through the chow line: "I would like to speak to you. I would like to ask for your help." Her large eyes looked at me as though she were terrified. It must have taken a great effort for her to ask.

I told her I'd meet her after she finished work that evening. Although, like most other 19-year-olds on the base or anywhere in the occupation for that matter, I kept hoping to meet a woman who would fulfill all the fantasies Hollywood had created for us, this didn't even cross my mind in relation to Adele. I felt there was something more serious, more profound in meeting her.

During dinner that evening I kept glancing across the dining hall at her, impatiently trying to find some clue as to what she wanted, even as I chatted with the other men at my table and listened to the orchestra, which varied day to day from three to five instruments, strings, brass and woodwinds.

It was a pretty good orchestra for an enlisted men's mess hall.

It was unusual that it was there at all; in most other outfits only the officer's mess had the luxury of live music. The problem with this orchestra, from the soldiers' standpoint, was that it principally played classical music, concentrating on the baroque and the waltz, with occasional pieces of symphonies or opera. Nary a "Mairzy Doats" or "Beer Barrel Polka," and except for perfunctory polite applause at the end of each performance, there was little acknowledgment of the musicians' skills. They must have felt that their art was in vain. That evening they played one classical piece that instantly became a part of their daily repertoire.

It was one of those days when the men were preoccupied with griping about the food, which that evening consisted mainly of leftovers, and they paid even less attention than usual to the orchestra. The musicians seemed dispirited too, and in order to liven things up began a spirited excerpt from a standard classical piece they hadn't played before.

Suddenly the atmosphere in the mess hall changed. The GIs began clapping and shouting, and as the music reached a crescendo, so did their reaction. The musicians, their faces bubbling with smiles of satisfaction, played exultantly as the acclaim grew and they heard echoing through the dining hall shouts of "Hoch! Hoch! Hoch!" and "Hooray!" When the musicians finished they stepped forward to take bows for the first time, as the GIs continued to cheer and pound on the tables. Most mealtimes after that the orchestra included that piece, with the same overwhelming response. The musicians began to anticipate it, their faces bathed in confidence each time they began. They must have thought that somehow, in that particular piece of music, all their talents magically blended together to reach the summit of their artistry. For years afterward they could tell themselves that rarely in the history of music, even for the most renowned symphony orchestras, was there such uninhibited approval. I wondered if the musicians would someday learn the real meaning and stimulation to the GIs of the piece they were playing, the finale of Rossini's "William Tell Overture," and that what sounded like a German approval, "Hoch! Hoch!" and the American "Hooray!" was in fact the shout of "Hi-ho, Silver, away!" I hope they never found out. There is little enough glory for an artist in a lifetime.

Adele asked me to come home with her because she wanted me to meet someone. While I was keenly aware of the warnings to GIs not to go off alone with a woman, I had no concern about Adele. She clearly was both more and less than she seemed, and I was certain that none of it was bad. She kept several feet from me, more fearful than I was, as we crossed the footbridge over the narrow woodsy area that separated the road in front of the air base from a small residential section. The center of Kaufbeuren was a mile away down a winding hill from the several blocks of two-story, white, wooden frame houses lived in by middle-class Germans who were mostly shopkeepers and white collar workers in town. Many of the homeowners took in roomers, the extra money helpful in buying some of the necessities that were available only on the black market at inflated prices. Some of the roomers were displaced persons, but as long as their papers showed they weren't Jews, they were welcomed out of necessity. What little food they could get they ate in their rooms, cooking with electric hot plates or small Sterno stoves.

We walked for about ten minutes along a path bordered by the multicolored flowers of Bavarian springtime and arrived at the entrance to the second floor of one of the small houses. The door was opened by a slim young woman with sparkling dark eyes and a small round mouth, her face framed by shining brown hair. She was introduced as Miriam, her papers showing her first name as Maria and a different last name than Adele's, but listing her as well as a Catholic from Poland, 17 years of age.

"We are sisters," Adele told me.

"But you have different names?"

"These are false papers," they told me. "False names. Christian names. Otherwise they would have shipped us to a camp. We are Jews."

Even with the war over and the Nazis war machine defeated, it took courage to reveal that one was a Jew.

I learned later that their ages were also different. Miriam, who looked older, was 16; Adele, who looked younger, was 17.

"Adele has told me about you," Miriam said to me. "That you seem very kind. That she thinks we can trust you."

We spoke in German, as best as I was able. Although there were many words I didn't know, I think we all understood the essence of what we were saying.

They told me their parents were in America. "We don't know whether they are dead or alive. They don't know whether we are dead or alive. We want to find them, but we don't know how. Will you help us?"

They told me their story. In 1938 their parents were brought to America by an older son who was already in this country, and

made arrangements for Miriam and Adele, then nine and ten, another son and a married daughter with a year-old child to join them
from their town of Zamosc, near Lublin. In the summer of 1939
their immigration visas were granted. On September 1, 1939, just
as they were preparing to leave for America, Germany invaded Poland. It was too late.

Within weeks the Germans had reached Lublin. The two
young girls, along with their brother and sister and all the other
Jews from their town, were taken to the outskirts of Lublin. There
the Jews was forced to dig a long trench, long enough to accommodate the bodies of all those who dug and deep enough to cover the
bodies with dirt. After the self-made graves were completed, the
diggers had to strip completely. Machine guns manned by German
soldiers were turned on them and they were ruthlessly killed, then
their bodies pushed into the trenches and covered over with dirt
by the next group to be murdered. On this particular day, as the
guns began to fire, some of the intended victims began to run in a
last-second attempt to hide in the nearby woods and perhaps escape immediate death. The girls' brother was killed outright, while
Adele and Miriam and their sister with her child hid in the brush.
The German soldiers roamed the woods with their guns blazing,
not wanting to lose a single corpse in their game of death. The two
girls heard their sister's baby cry. The Germans must have heard
the crying too, because several seconds later there was the sound
of shots and no more crying. Miraculously, Adele and Miriam were
not found.

For months they hid with non-Jewish friends, who eventually got them false papers out of Poland and into Russia.

"Our biggest fear in Russia was not the Germans," Miriam told me. "They hadn't come that far yet. It was when I had a terrible pain in my side and I had to go to a hospital and they said I had appendicitis. I wasn't afraid of the operation. I was afraid that under the ether I might say something that would let them know we were Jews." She would tell that story often in later years, the incongruity making it seem more humorous than fearful.

In the winter of the German defeat at Stalingrad in 1943, as the German Army pulled back, the girls were split up and shipped out of Russia as slave laborers. Miriam was sent to Italy and assigned as a *putzmadchen*, a cleaning woman in an army hospital kitchen. She was occasionally given additional assignments, such as helping the hospital staff comfort the gravely wounded; she later recalled the irony of a Jewish girl consoling Nazi soldiers. Before she left, she was able to give Adele her *Feldpost* address.

Adele was sent to Romania and eventually was taken to Germany, where she worked as a slave laborer in factories, offices and shops. Although both girls wrote to each other weekly, no mail got through except one postcard from Adele to Miriam in 1944 saying she was in a small town in Germany near Stuttgart. Miriam's field hospital unit retreated from Italy to Germany and by the war's end was established in a convent near Kaufbeuren.

At the new hospital base near Kaufbeuren, Miriam and the other non-Germans, mostly Russian women, continued to live and work under intolerable conditions. Even when the war ended, the German doctors and nurses treated them as if they were still slaves. Not only did they get very little food, but three were forced to sleep in a five by ten foot room. Miriam decided to complain about their treatment to the Kaufbeuren military command. The person who received the complaint, a Lieutenant Lee, offered no help. One of the D.P. employees in the office, a Mrs. Milner, who was Jewish, sympathized and personally went to the hospital head to complain. The hospital chief objected to what he felt was undue interference and complained to Lieutenant Lee, who severely censured Mrs. Milner, especially for bothering at all with D.P.s.

Miriam told Mrs. Milner that she was Jewish, a risky admission at that time. Mrs. Milner—she and her husband, who was murdered by the Nazis, had been university professors before the war—took her under her wing and introduced her to a sympathetic senior military officer. He invited her to dinner at this home. This same officer and Mrs. Milner subsequently arranged with the mother superior of the convent for decent quarters for Miriam in the convent.

In the meantime Miriam had received no further word from Adele and decided to try to find her. Because there was no other transportation available, she walked and hitchhiked to Stuttgart, about 110 miles to the northwest, joining the tens of thousands who crowded the roads. When Miriam arrived in the suburb where she believed her sister was, she walked the streets wondering how to find her. Then she noticed a handwritten menu posted on the door of a tavern and recognized Adele's distinctive handwriting. Miriam asked for her "cousin" by the name on Adele's false papers. The barmaid yelled upstairs, and in a moment the two girls were hugging in a tearful reunion. After a few days they both went to Kaufbeuren, where Adele was permitted to share Miriam's room in the convent.

When Adele arrived in Kaufbeuren, she went immediately to the MG office for proper registration, ration cards and living quarters, all due displaced persons under orders issued by SHAEF in Paris. She was permitted to speak only to the young German woman who was Lieutenant Lee's interpreter—she did not see Mrs. Milner—and was told to leave Kaufbeuren immediately and go back to Stuttgart. She didn't. When Adele got the job at the U.S. base, they rented their room in the private house.

"We want to see our parents again," they told me. "We want to join them in America. But we don't know how to find them."

Despite what they had been through, they both seemed small and helpless, like the children they had not been allowed to be for the past six years.

"We'll find them," I promised. "We'll find them."

I encouraged them to obtain proper identification papers so that when we located their parents it would be possible for them to obtain the necessary immigration credentials. Because they lived in the Kaufbeuren district, they had no choice but to go back to Lieutenant Lee. They explained the reason for the false papers they had carried for five years and their need for proper identifying documents. Lieutenant Lee refused to act on their request, telling them they had no proof of their claimed identities. I then went with them to see Lieutenant Lee to argue on their behalf. He did not question my explanation, but still refused to give them papers in their correct names showing they were Jewish.

"Why?" I asked.

His answer, curt and matter-of-fact: "They don't look Jewish."

Hundreds of D.P.s who came for help to the Kaufbeuren MG

were treated the same way, and dozens of Americans witnessed such treatment. The Kaufbeuren MG and Lieutenant Lee were not unique. They were microcosms of the military government operations in many parts of the American-occupied zone. Lee's interpreter and secretary had been entrusted with many of the operations of the office. She was good-looking and German. It was generally believed her duties went far beyond secretarial. She was an active pro-Nazi, according to D.P.s who dealt with her, and she made things particularly miserable for D.P.s, especially any Jews who came for help. She gave assistance to many Germans; Nazis were given special favors. She openly insulted displaced persons and her translations were primarily oriented to her political purposes, with accuracy usually incidental. Complaints to Lieutenant Lee brought no action. Finally, after many complaints to the area military headquarters in Munich, an order came to Lee to fire her because of her continuing Nazi activity. Although the military government believed the Kaufbeuren MG could get along without this resident Nazi, apparently Lieutenant Lee could not, and after a short while he rehired her and gave her the same measure of power she had had before.

Not only did some individual MG officers continue their own form of genocide by neglect against the survivors and displaced persons, some of the orders from SHAEF made it easier for them to do so. One such order took away from D.P.s any special status or treatment in Germany. They were given the alternative of either returning to their native lands or living "on the economy" in Germany, under the control of the Germans, without direct aid from the U.S. That was indeed a Hobson's choice.

Thousands of *auslander*—many at the point of a gun—were forced by the American forces into trains and boxcars that took them to points of concentration, and after many had been relieved of all their baggage, including food, drink, clothing and keepsakes, they were herded into further conveyances, principally large trucks, and transported to their native lands. This action helped solve for the American military government some of the problems of providing supplies. With more food and clothing available, Germans now had more rations than the people of most of the countries they had ravaged, and whose families and friends they had murdered.

Some six weeks after this policy was put into effect, the U.S. high command realized it had made a mistake, and the order was rescinded. Those D.P.s who had escaped deportation now were given a greater food allotment and, in some areas, greater opportunity for housing. But the harm had been done.

Under the deportation policy, Lieutenant Lee once came to the base to personally direct the deportation of a former slave laborer working there who wanted to stay in Germany in order to try to get to England or the United States; she did not want to go back to Hungary because her entire family had been killed. He flatly denied her request and forcibly sent her to Hungary. As a newspaper editor ostensibly covering a story on the base, I asked him what he thought of D.P.s. His answer was that there was not a single "good" D.P. among the hundreds of thousands who were at that time still in the American zone of occupation. He was certain that all they did was cause trouble, and he did not hesitate to tell me the problems they made for him.

A number of D.P.s and American soldiers, myself included,

reported Lieutenant Lee's prejudicial attitudes and actions to the regional military government headquarters in Munich. Several months later the MG headquarters took action: It promoted Lieutenant Lee to Captain.

# Chapter 5 ❦

## FOOD . . . AND MORE

While cigarettes were the most precious commodity for most Germans, who used them as barter for hard-to-come-by necessities, food was the most precious commodity for the survivors at St. Ottilien, as well as at other displaced persons camps. Although SHAEF had ordered rations of 1,200 calories per day for each D.P. in the camps under American jurisdiction, most received 600 calories or less. While 600 was, in fact, more than they had received in the German concentration camps, 1,200 calories was considered the minimum to maintain satisfactory health. The food was available. It simply didn't reach most of the survivors. Some of it disappeared on the way from Paris, at key distribution points in Europe, sold on the black market by the American soldiers transporting it. Some was diverted when it reached the military government headquarters at its point of destination, allocated to favored German civilians. Some was deliberately withheld from the survivors by the Military Police (MPs) charged with distributing food at the camps; they sold it on the black market, gave it to a German mistress or two, or bartered it to survivors in exchange for sex.

Most of the people in most of the camps were starving, and at St. Ottilien the lack of food for people who were in debilitated physical condition, some seriously ill, meant not only deprivation, but death.

Virtually all the help the survivors at St. Ottilien got was unofficial, from individual officers and enlisted men at nearby bases who had heard of the hospital and the plight of its patients, and wanted to help.

Probably the most dedicated American in this category was an army chaplain, Captain Abraham J. Klausner, who became the unofficial rabbi to the Jewish survivors at St. Ottilien, serving as a psychological as much as a spiritual adviser. Klausner devoted unstinting time and effort to the needs of St. Ottilien. He organized searches for food and clothing, not only going to the military government headquarters in Munich for help, but seeking out whatever aid he could at nearby cities, towns and villages. He went to army camps to let the U.S. soldiers know of the situation at St. Ottilien and ask for their help.

One of Klausner's important contributions was in organizing searches for missing relatives. His efforts led to the compilation of five volumes listing the names of the survivors who were in D.P. camps in the American zones in Germany and Austria. He distributed these lists to army chaplains—Jewish and non-Jewish—who took them to the various camps to try to reconnect families and friends who, miraculously, were still alive.

Attempts by St. Ottilien to get official help were futile. Dr. Grinberg wrote many times to virtually every organization in Europe and the United States that ostensibly had as its mission assistance to those in need, including—and in some cases, especially or exclusively—Holocaust survivors. At best, the various organizations, including some that had raised funds in the United States, principally from Jewish sources for the purpose of helping the survivors, gave only lip service.

Naively, Dr. Grinberg and the leaders of some of the other survivor camps thought that help would be forthcoming in response to letters pleading for aid, such as the following one to the World Jewish Congress:

> May 31, 1945
>
> We, the surviving Jews of Europe, appeal to you as the central agency of the Jewish people. Four weeks have passed since our liberation and no single representative of any Jewish organization has come to speak with us concerning what happened to us in the most horrible persecution that has ever transpired, to give us comfort, to alleviate our need or to bring us aid. We have had to help ourselves with our own poor strength. This has been our first great disappointment since our liberation and it is a fact that we cannot understand.
>
> Two questions torment us: Each of us burns with the wish to find out the tragic facts about his own family. We ask you therefore to send us as speedily as possible lists of the Jewish survivors in the Soviet and the German-occupied territories. We must know for whom to say Kaddish. The second question is: What will become of us? Where will they send us? Where will we have to continue our misery?
>
> We await your speedy reply and send you Zion's greetings in the hope that you will send us tradi-

tional Jewish brotherly aid in the time of our grav-
est need.
[signed]
Z. Grinberg, St. Ottilien
S. Gringauz, Landsberg
A. Bergmann, Munich

They were doomed to more than disappointment; they were
doomed to watch more and more of the survivors die.

At the Kaufbeuren air base a number of sympathetic soldiers
tried various ploys to obtain food and get it to St. Ottilien. The
easiest approach was to save food from our meals at the mess hall,
from purchases of candy and cookies and other small packages of
food at the Post Exchange (the PX was the commissary where service men and women could buy specified, limited amounts of personal articles such as toiletries, some items of clothing, cigarettes,
soft drinks and some foods), from packages of food sent from home
(hard salamis were a favorite item) and, as it turned out, the most
dependable source, food stolen from army kitchens.

We had no compunction about the latter. Most of the GIs
who worked in the kitchens took food for their own purposes, usually for their German mistresses. In fact, the mess sergeant openly
bragged about his mother-daughter combination, and it was common knowledge that substantial amounts of food were going for
the upkeep of his harem.

One of the most contradictory personalities and at the same
time one of the most helpful men at the base was Frankie Kline.
He was in his 30s, perhaps as much as 35, and was considered an

old man by us 18-, 19- and 20-year-olds. But his thin, wiry body and lean face were perpetually full of energy and he often seemed younger than we did. Frankie worked in the kitchen and would know how to smuggle food to St. Ottilien.

He had told us that he'd worked for a bootlegger when he was a kid in New York and had even been in jail. He hated the army. More than most. He was one of the nonconformists of the Second Wing who had served time in an army prison. He didn't tell us much more, but we assumed it was the prison at Camp Edwards in Massachusetts, where a number of others in the Second Wing had been incarcerated. Its formal name was the East Coast Processing Center, or ECPC. We pronounced it in one word: "eeseepeesee." The army concentration camp, according to those who had been there. The "black box," "the hole" and other forms of discipline and torture not only broke men but sometimes killed them. The American press revealed the horrors of the prison for court-martialed American soldiers at Litchfield, England, but has never made known what went on on our own shores.

We were never sure why Frankie was in eeseepeesee. He let on that he had been AWOL for three years after being drafted at the beginning of the war. Now he was here, along with the rest of the rebels, misfits and chip-on-the-shoulder ex-infantrymen and the fly boys who spent the war in warm beds in England, here in this conglomerate outfit of souvenir hunters. They didn't know what to do with Frankie. But he knew. "Put me in the kitchen," he said. Whatever else happened, this kid from the slums of Brooklyn was going to get enough to eat.

When you wanted something done, you went to the

eeseepeesee graduates. Most of them cared more about people than about rules. Many of them came from backgrounds where the great American dream eluded them because the rules for playing were stacked against them to begin with. When you've been deprived yourself, it's sometimes easier to understand and do something for others who are deprived. When I told Frankie about St. Ottilien, he was more than willing.

"Can you get a car?" he asked me. "A big, closed one?"

I thought I could requisition one of the large touring cars that had been left behind on the Kaufbeuren air base.

"Are they all Jews?" Frankie asked.

"Almost all. Some communists who aren't. Some political prisoners who helped the Jews or opposed Hitler."

"Holy mother," he laughed. "Commies and Jews. My fucking parish priest would shit in his pants if he knew I was helping commies and Jews. He's the bastard who wouldn't do nothing to help me when I was arrested and sent to jail as a kid. Commies and kikes! Would I like to tell that to the old bastard's face!"

My roommate and assistant editor on the *2nd Wing Eagle* was Anthony "Dee" DiBiase. Dee had come to the Second Wing after spending time in eeseepeesee. He had completed basic training and got a final leave home to Philadelphia before his outfit shipped out overseas. While at home he got pneumonia, and an army doctor gave him medication and told him to stay home until the doctor revisited him and told him it was all right to rejoin his outfit. He didn't hear from the doctor again and for the next thirteen months stayed at home and got married. A neighbor whose son was in the service angrily called the army, the Military Police came and got

Dee, and he was court-martialed and sent to eeseepeesee.

Dee had finished vocational high school, had never been to college and had never worked on a newspaper. I welcomed him both on the newspaper and as my roommate. He was open and honest with me, and I could be the same with him. Dee's quick wit and talent at drawing converted colloquial language into good newspaper humor and army gripes into biting cartoons.

I told him about St. Ottilien.

"Those poor bastards. As bad as you say, huh?"

"Worse."

"We all got our troubles."

"Some got it worse."

"Yeah, but you get too involved in other people's troubles and sometimes you end up worse than they are," Dee said.

"Or better."

"Bullshit!" He paused a moment. "Those people in St. Ottilien, they really had it bad, didn't they?"

"No shit!"

"Fuck you too." Dee lay down on his bed. "We oughta be able to scrounge up some food for them."

I told him that Frankie was going to smuggle some food out of the mess hall and that I had put in for a car from the motor pool. "We're going to do it tomorrow," I told him.

"Well, I ain't got nothing important to do tomorrow. I'll come along on the deal." He turned off the light and pulled a blanket over his head.

"Dee, you *chudruhl*, you don't fool me."

"Go to sleep."

The next day, after lunch, we drove the car to the back door of the mess hall. It was a touring car that had been abandoned at the base by the Germans and had probably been used to drive high-ranking officers when they visited.

"I'm ready to load up," Frankie said. "Cookie's out fucking his mother-daughter team."

"The sonuvabitch is looting the place blind," I complained, "and we've got to sneak stuff out to people who really need it."

That was one of the ways food got to St. Ottilien.

E. Edward Herman may have been the only GI ever to buy out an entire PX. Ed Herman, although only a private, was already making more money through business deals while in the army than any of us had made in civilian life. Ed was 25, from Philadelphia and had begun his college career at the University of Pennsylvania as a football player. When the war started, he left school to become a partner in a small plant subcontracting defense materiel, and also became a partner in a ballroom that planned to bring name bands to Philadelphia. Before joining the Second Wing he had been stationed near Paris with the U.S. Strategic Air Force. A disagreement with a captain resulted in his transfer to Kaufbeuren.

Shortly after he arrived in Kaufbeuren, Ed got together every cent he could, arranged a pass to Paris with the blessing of the commanding colonel's office for the purpose of buying goods that could not be found in Germany and that could be made available in the PX for Second Wing personnel to send back home. Specifically, he brought back French perfumes, giving a number of bottles to the officers who had made possible his shopping trip and putting the remainder on sale in the PX. Ed probably didn't make any

money on this first deal, but his largesse and the heightened morale on the base in getting French perfumes for German mistresses,
or in some cases sent to wives and sweethearts back home, convinced the colonel to send him on more such missions. France, just
beginning its recovery from the war, had been stripped bare. It was
eager for the kinds of consumer goods that Germany had been
manufacturing. Even with the factories in the Third Reich having
been dedicated to war production, many still had stockpiles of consumer goods, and some had begun producing them again. French
entrepreneurs had also begun producing the kinds of goods they
had previously marketed to Germany.

There was no mechanism yet for the trade that business
people on both sides of the border wanted. Both the French government and the U.S. Military Government in Germany kept tight
controls on all movement between the countries. The principal way
goods could be sold or exchanged was through black market operations or through operations such as Ed's.

He began to use the trips on behalf of the PX for two-way
commerce. He went anywhere for anything that had market value.
In the Black Forest of southern Germany he bought up cuckoo
clocks. He sold the clocks in Paris, setting up an account in a bank
there. In Germany he bought watches to be sold in France, and in
France cosmetics to be sold in Germany. He got Paris hats, lingerie
and other fashions that brought a good price in Germany, and cameras, optical equipment and precision medical instruments from
Germany. He even arranged with music stores in Paris to buy a
shipment of Hohner harmonicas that had become exhausted in the
world markets during the war but were still available in Germany.

Once, when it was necessary to conceal the goods he was carrying and avoid inspection of his vehicle, Ed arranged to use the base ambulance. In addition, he always carried enough money and samples of the scarce goods he was transporting to bribe the border guards when necessary.

Edward had two credos. The first was that he was willing to invest 99 cents to make a dollar, with sufficient volume making it worth his while. The second was his vow that he would be a millionaire before he was 30. And he was—more than once. After the war he became wealthy working in international finance. Ed had joined me in visiting St. Ottilien and bringing in food. Sometimes he brought even more exotic items such as toothpaste, shaving cream, razor blades, patent medicines such as aspirin and Alka Seltzer, even candy that he managed to get from the PX, despite the strict rationing for each soldier.

After a couple of months, the PX at the Kaufbeuren air base was shut down for expansion and reorganization. That gave Ed an idea. Rather than store its entire inventory for the expected six-week hiatus, during which much of the provisions would spoil, perhaps the PX would be willing to sell its stock directly to Ed? He would then have a bonanza to deliver to St. Ottilien. Cans of juices, soft drinks, candy bars, boxes of crackers, toothbrushes and toothpaste, shaving cream and razor blades, soap, socks, shirts and other goods. Not enough food to appreciably improve the survivors' diet, but enough special items to be of some help. Toiletries like lotions would be of special value to the morale of both the men and women. And lots of chewing gum for the children.

I was nonplused by Ed's suggestion. "You can't buy a PX!"

"Why not?"

"Well . . . it's just not done. Did you ever hear of it being done? How can you just go in and buy a PX?"

"I don't see why I can't," Ed said.

To this day I don't know quite how he did it. With the blessing of PX officer Lieutenant Albert L. Cusick, who was active in trying to help the displaced persons, Ed made the altruistic investment. He became perhaps the only U.S. Armed Forces serviceman in history to personally buy out a PX. It cost him $450, not much by today's standards, but a considerable sum at a time when $50 per week was considered a good salary in the U.S., and when $10 a week could support a family in occupied Germany. Among the items he bought were 10 cases of fruit juices, 1,950 candy bars, 600 bars of Lux soap, toothbrushes, shaving cream, razor blades and towels. Colonel Charles B. Tyler, who was commanding officer of the base, not only knew about the transaction, but somehow Ed was able to obtain his full cooperation. The colonel even provided Ed with a car to deliver the goods.

The people at St. Ottilien were happier than we had seen them before. For the first time in years they got more than the necessities for survival—personal articles that at that moment took on the aura of luxury items. There were toiletries that few of the patients had even remotely expected to have any time in the near future.

Even those seriously ill in their beds smiled and mustered enough energy to say thank you in the strongest, clearest voices they could as we gave them a bar of soap, a toothbrush and toothpaste, a shirt and socks and, with permission of the doctors, one or two candy bars. We saved the bottles of men's after shave and co-logne for the women. It was the closest thing in years they'd had to perfume.

Some of the light clothing would be useful up to the time when the weather would begin to get really cold. And the hospital now had more aspirin, alcohol and handkerchiefs (to use for ban-dages) than it had received up to that time.

A few of us sat around one evening talking about Ed Herman's largesse. We marveled at his business acumen and his ability to pull off a deal we would have thought impossible under any circumstances. Those of us who had been doing what we could to help the people at St. Ottilien were euphoric to have Ed's coup rub off on us, as baseball fans revel in the success of their home team as if they them-selves had hit the homeruns and pitched the shutouts.

We were youth, having done what was easy for us, our small and short-range goals readily accomplished, breathing in success, sometimes dealing with even the most serious problems of life as though we were in a game, feeling that nothing was lasting and that everything was eternal; joyous, fresh youth in our own world that transcended the division between reality and fantasy, filling our glasses with liquor made in some unknown bathtub by some unknown hand in some unknown city in a strange land, losing our-selves, naturally and freely, to our own pinpoint moments of irre-sponsibility. Intellectually aware of St. Ottilien, emotionally re-moved from it when we wished to be, we were like the pilots who went into battle for an hour or two and then left the war behind for another day for clean sheets, a hot meal, whiskey and women and a chorus of Tipperary around a piano, while the people of St. Ottilien were like the dogfaces who came out of their holes in the ground for C-rations and coffee, and went back into them with their breaths caught in their throats, their bodies shaking cold with fear, their skin tight and hard and prickly, knowing without cessation twenty-four hours of every day that the war was not in front of them or in back of them but continuously and constantly around them and in the middle of them and not for a second able to erase from their minds and feelings that the next second could be without warning their last second of life.

So we laughed and joked and filled our glasses with bathtub scotch and drank as if the only reality in life was that carefree existence we created at that very moment in that room. We made toasts to Ed and to each other.

"Ed's gotta be the best wheeler-dealer in the world," Dee said. "Who else could buy out a PX?"

"With a heart of gold," I added.

Edward Herman could have made a bundle by selling the PX goods on the black market. It all went to St. Ottilien. Even some of the cigarettes. It was extremely generous of Ed to include cigarettes. At the time, we didn't know that the last thing these sick and dying people needed was to smoke cigarettes to speed them on their way to the grave. I always wondered whether Ed tried to make up part of his philanthropy by selling on the black market the cigarettes that he didn't give to St. Ottilien.

Another, although not usual, way we got food for St. Ottilien was by intimidating German authorities who had access to food that was distributed to their civilian sector through the military government.

On occasion I would ask Dr. Grinberg what kinds of food we should try to get for St. Ottilien.

"Protein."

"And?"

"Something heavy. Starch. Like potatoes."

"Real potatoes, you mean? Not the powdered potatoes from the base."

He nodded.

"How much do you need immediately?"

"A hundred pounds could feed everybody. Potato soup, potato pancakes, potato stew, potato with some greens from the field."

"It is difficult to find real potatoes," I said. "But I'll try."

I borrowed the uniform of Lieutenant Jack Manheim, one of the officers who had been most active in finding supplies for the survivors at St. Ottilien. To make any impression on a German official I knew I needed an officer's uniform, including the fly-boy hat. To avoid violating any army regulations, I carefully removed the officer's insignia. I gambled that the Germans wouldn't notice the difference. I drove to the office of the Bürgermeister in the town of Buchloe, not far from St. Ottilien. Dressed in an officer's uniform borrowed from Lieutenant Cusick—also with insignia removed—Dee went with me.

The Bürgermeister's secretary, assuming we were officers, ushered us in immediately. I walked in rigidly, snapping my boot heels against the wooden floor, my face tight and impatient, my eyebrows tilted just enough to indicate the superiority of disdain. As seriously as I improvised this Hollywood stereotype of the Nazi officer, I had to hold back a smile as I realized the irony of the

Bürgermeister accepting my manner as real. It was kind of fun pretending to be Erich Von Stroheim. I wondered if the Bürgermeister had seen *Grand Illusion* too.

Dee, who neither spoke nor understood any German, followed a few steps behind to give the impression that I was important enough to have an aide along. I walked directly up to the Bürgermeister's desk, nodded curtly at him as he began to rise to greet me and in my best guttural accent announced, *"Ich muss früh am Morgen hundert pfunt Kartoffeln haben."*

While my two years of studying German in high school did not qualify me to hold an intellectual conversation or to be even passably literate in grammar and tense, I knew enough German to communicate what I wanted. To the Germans, used to Americans who neither spoke nor understood a word of German, French or any of the other languages that most Europeans knew, I appeared not only comparatively literate but perhaps even highly educated.

The Bürgermeister stood stark still, taken aback not only by my unexpected demand for a hundred pounds of potatoes by the following morning, but by my departure from the usual American cordial introduction and casual chat before getting down to business.

He nodded at a chair near his desk, saw that I was not going to sit, wasn't sure whether he ought to sit or stand, remained in a half-crouching position for a moment, then decided he would have to stand because I did.

Half-apologetically, but with as convincing a tone as he could muster, he said there were no potatoes available in Buchloe. He repeated it, more to reinforce the statement than to make sure I understood. *"Es gibt keine Kartoffeln im Buchloe."*

I took a long pause, lifted my head and tried to look down the edge of my nose at him. *"Sind Sie nicht der Bürgermeister?"*

*"Jawohl."*

*"Ich habe Kartoffeln im Buchloe gesehen. Was für ein Bürgermeister sind Sie dass wenn Sie nicht sehen was anderen Menchen sehen ganz offensichtlich?"*

My questioning the kind of a Bürgermeister he was not to know of the availability of potatoes in his own city, when I knew there were some, worried him. Both his integrity and his competence were being challenged. He insisted that there really were no potatoes available, but if he ever got any, he would let me know.

*"Wenn Ich Kartoffeln knieben kann, werde Ich die ihnen garne zukommen lassen, aber jetzt es gibt keine Kartoffeln."*

With deliberate casualness, emphasizing each word, I told him that maybe we needed a different Bürgermeister, one better able to requisition potatoes. *"Veleicht Wir brauchen einen starkeren Bürgermeister der Kartoffeln auftreiben kann?"*

I whirled before he could answer, started out, turned back at the door: *"Ich will Morgen am acht Uhr hier sein. Erwarte Ich hundert pfundt Kartoffeln auszufinden. Egal wie sie die auftreiben."* I clicked my heels, slapped my right hand against my thigh, wondered whether the Bürgermeister had seen Conrad Veidt in *Casablanca* and marched out of the office. Dee followed me and, embellishing the drama of the moment, slammed the door hard behind him.

"What the hell was that all about?" Dee asked when we got outside.

"The sonuvabitch insisted there were no potatoes anywhere around. But I said I knew there were and that maybe another mayor might be more efficient in locating them. I told him we'd be back tomorrow morning at eight. I bet there's a hundred pounds of potatoes waiting."

There was. The Bürgermeister had two large burlap sacks full of potatoes.

*"Ich habe die ganzen Nacht gearbeitet,"* he said. *"Das ist alles was Ich auftreiben konnte."* Even if he did work the entire night getting all the potatoes available in Buchloe—which I knew was a lie—I couldn't have cared less, and I gave no sign of either sympathy or appreciation.

I abruptly handed him a piece of paper to sign that stated that the potatoes were being voluntarily donated by his office to the D.P. hospital at St. Ottilien. *"Bitte,"* I said to him, more in the tone of an order than a request. He signed the paper; I took it, slowly and deliberately folded it and put it in my outside pocket.

Without even a thank you to the Bürgermeister, I motioned to him to have the sacks brought outside to my jeep. Two young Germans carried them out under the supervision of the Bürgermeister. I got in the car, stared at him a moment, said, *"Das gefehlt mir,"* to let him know I was pleased, in case I wanted to hit him up for more food at a future time, and drove off. The Bürgermeister seemed not quite to know whether I was appreciative or angry. "Let him worry," I said to myself. "It'll be easier the next time I want potatoes."

When I delivered the potatoes to St. Ottilien I told Dr. Grinberg about the encounter with the Bürgermeister and laughed at my own chutzpah. "I went in to the Bürgermeister acting like a Nazi officer and within twenty-four hours we got the potatoes."

I remember that Dr. Grinberg didn't even smile.

# Chapter 6 ⌒

# Good News

Some good things did happen.

We tried every way possible to locate Miriam and Adele's parents. The only things the sisters knew for certain was that their oldest brother was a tailor and that before the war he had been living and working in Brooklyn. That's where their parents had gone. But after the war started there was no way either their brother or parents could make further contact with them, and they had no way of reaching anyone in America.

One of the officers on the base, Captain Maxwell Kirchner, had visited St. Ottilien and had taken it upon himself to try to locate and contact any known relatives of the survivors anyplace in the world. He succeeded in finding a number of them, who subsequently arranged for their kin at St. Ottilien to emigrate to their countries.

But he was unable to locate the sisters' parents or brother. They could not be found in any of the New York City boroughs' phone directories. The telephone business pages did not list their brother under "tailors." The New York newspaper *P.M.* daily ran lists of the names of survivors in Europe who were seeking relatives in the United States, and we sent in a notice with the sisters' names, city where they had lived before the war and the relatives they were seeking. That didn't work. We put a paid ad in the *New York Post* and a notice in the *Jewish Daily Forward*. No response. We contacted all the Jewish organizations we could locate in New York and asked them to try to find the parents. None were successful.

We were beginning to think our quest was futile when a remarkable coincidence occurred. Lieutenant Jack Manheim's parents, to whom he had written about the sisters and the attempts to locate their family, were attending a wedding in New York. At the wedding dinner, they told the story of the sisters to others at their table. One man observed that the secretary of his *Landsmanschaften*—a society that looked after burial needs, weddings and arranged social gatherings for émigrés from the same town or area—had the same last name as the sisters, was from the same part of Poland and had family members who had been left behind when the war started. At two o'clock in the morning they called Morris Schiff. Indeed, he was Miriam and Adele's older brother. He was working in the garment industry and had moved with his parents from Brooklyn to the Bronx several years earlier.

What excitement on the base when Jack Manheim came running to the sisters that very morning, waving a telegram from New York saying that their family had been found! Laughter and joy and tears. Their parents quickly began the process of getting permission for their immigration to the States. While U.S. immigration policies were extremely restrictive, exceptions were made for concentration camp survivors and displaced persons, including Jews, who had blood relatives living in the States who would guarantee responsibility for them once they were admitted.

Now it was important that we get them accurate credentials, in their right names, so we could seek authorization from the State Department office at the military government headquarters in Munich for them to go to an immigration center in Germany and then to a port of embarkation to board a ship to the United States.

As soon as we received the documents from America showing that their parents were in fact residents of the United States and Miriam and Adele were eligible to migrate there to join them, we were able to get the new identification papers. I then took the documents to Munich and showed them to the State Department official. He had only recently arrived in Munich to screen applicants for entry to the U.S. He refused to even look at the papers and summarily dismissed me, telling me to come back in a couple of weeks because he did not yet have his office set up properly to do business. He had learned fast, I thought. His manner was identical to the imperious brush-off practiced by so many military government officers. The next time I went to see him I asked Ed Herman to come with me. The official's behavior was the same. This time he said to come back in another couple of weeks because he did not yet have the official State Department documents or seal necessary to provide the authorization. I was ready to blow up, but Ed knew better how to handle the situation. In his very polite, matter-of-fact way, Ed treated our request as a formal transaction that of course would be completed when we returned in two weeks.

When Ed and I went back again, the State Department representative attempted to put us off once more. "I still don't have paper to write on," he insisted. "I don't even have a pen to write with."

That was too much for even Ed's usual controlled, calm exterior. When Ed got angry, he could be frightening. He had the build of a football player, and although I never saw Ed engage in any physical violence, he looked like someone you didn't want to tangle with. He glared at the official, who immediately began to back away.

Ed slowly and deliberately walked toward him. "What do you mean you don't have paper or pen?" Ed demanded as he moved closer to the man, standing just a few inches from him. I thought Ed was going to grab him by the collar and thrash him. The man must have thought so too, because he began to quake. Since he was new to Europe, he might have feared that we were cold-blooded infantry veterans who would just as soon kill him as not. At the least, given Ed's threatening manner, he might expect a pretty good beating.

Ed took a pen out of his own pocket and grabbed a sheet of paper from the man's desk. "Here is a pen and here's paper. Is that what you need? Now go ahead and write whatever you have to write."

The man hurried to reassure Ed. "I'll do it. I've have it ready first thing tomorrow. Please come back tomorrow morning."

We did. To our surprise, he had the papers ready, signed, with the official State Department seal. We took them to Miriam and Adele, who were overjoyed. Now it was more than just a dream. When would they leave? It wasn't yet clear. They were on the State Department list. But there were so many eligible immigrants who had received their authorizations from various parts of Europe that the process might take many months. Miriam and Adele were obliged to check with the Munich office periodically, to find out when they could start their journey. For now they would just have to wait. As it turned out, many eligible immigrants languished in transient centers for two years and more before their turn came.

I met with Dr. Grinberg often during the ensuing months. Although I was not in any official position to do much more than commiserate, I unofficially continued to work with other soldiers to provide food and supplies to St. Ottilien. I did write letters—and delivered Dr. Grinberg's letters—to the military government headquarters in Munich detailing the difficult conditions of the survivors at St. Ottilien and asking for help.

Sometimes, when he had time, we would just sit and talk. I estimated that Dr. Grinberg was about 40, but I had only just turned 20, and our conversations were often father-to-son rather than man-to-man. While I affected an aura of confidence and strength, my childhood of growing up as the only Jewish kid in a strongly anti-Semitic neighborhood left me with a lot of insecurity and wariness. Dr. Grinberg saw this and attempted to bolster my ego. I would leave feeling better about myself, but also feeling some guilt that I was not able to reciprocate and somehow help him too.

One day he appeared to be very depressed.

"Are you ill?" I asked.

"I am sad. Always sad these days, thinking about my wife and son."

As he had told me earlier, shortly after the hospital was established at St. Ottilien, several of the healthier patients had been sent out as "runners" to the survivors' former countries and cities to see if any of their families were still alive and if there was any indication that they were, to see if they could be located. One had gone to Lithuania, to Dr. Grinberg's former home and neighbors. No one had seen his wife and son, Dr. Grinberg had told me, but the runner met one survivor who said he had seen them at one of the camps and had later heard that they had been exterminated.

I did something I hadn't done before: I put my arm across Dr. Grinberg's shoulder to comfort him, although still feeling much the child next to this man who had suffered so much and done so much to ease the suffering of others. He reached up and patted my hand. "You are a fine young man," he said. Then he corrected himself: "You are a fine man."

I was appreciative and uncomfortable at the same time. I withdrew my hand from his shoulder. Dr. Grinberg understood.

"You still don't feel sure of yourself," he said. "This is the first time you've tried to comfort me as a friend rather than acting like an acquaintance or someone who does not feel on an equal level."

I blushed and felt even more uncomfortable. "You can be proud of yourself as a man, not a boy," he said. "If you have doubts about yourself, think about St. Ottilien, think about what you have already done to save the lives of people here. See yourself as others see you."

"I tell myself that," I said, "but I am uncertain about so many things."

"Just be yourself," he told me. "Don't be afraid to act on your beliefs and your feelings in a personal way, just as you have not been afraid to do so in a public way and in a political way. Remember, you are at least as capable as the next person. Don't bend your knees to anyone."

I told him how much I appreciated his confidence and advice. "I feel what you say is true, but somehow I am never quite sure." I wanted to change the subject. I suggested that his wife and son might still be alive. No one had actually said they saw them go into the gas chambers, no one had actually seen them killed.

"It is several months since they would have been released, if they were alive," Dr. Grinberg said. "The runner left information that I was here at St. Ottilien. They would have gotten some word back to me by now." We talked about St. Ottilien then. His eyes were clear and his voice firm. He was determined to cast off his depression, to continue to find ways of helping those still alive. We talked about the increasingly urgent need for food, clothing and medicine, with the autumn chill already in the air. We knew that without help many or perhaps most of the people at St. Ottilien would not survive the winter. We talked about the same things we had talked about before.

Eisenhower's order that all D.P.s were to get 1,200 calories a day meant little, we decided. "Because we are not a regular D.P. camp, the military government authorities have said that we cannot get these rations. Not that it matters, because the regular D.P. camps aren't getting food either. The MPs in charge of the camps are using the food for black market, for bribery . . . for who knows what." He sighed. "Sometimes I think that the Americans have no more interest in our survival than the rest of the world."

He told me he had sent dozens of letters to relief organizations all over the world, including America and England. "You would think that maybe one of them would answer? None. Not one answer. Not even from the Jewish organizations."

In the middle of the conversation he suddenly stopped, remaining absolutely still. He moved only his eyes toward the door and stared as it opened and a woman came in followed by a boy. She looked at Dr. Grinberg, her face tight and wrinkled like those of the starving prisoners of the concentration camps. She tried to smile, then to laugh, but the sound became a plaintive wail as the tears poured from her eyes and her head shook up and down uncontrollably. It clearly was an effort for her to keep from sinking to the floor. The boy stood right behind her and stared at Dr. Grinberg with his eyes wide and his mouth open. Dr. Grinberg, still not moving, began crying, then moaning through his tears, "Oh, my God! Oh, my God!" over and over. Suddenly he pushed himself forward, took the woman into his arms, pulled the boy into his arms with her, began kissing the woman's face all over and did the same with the boy, his hands and arms moving all over them, around them, touching them, caressing them, making certain they were real, that they really were there.

I got out of my chair to leave, moving around them and out of their way.

Dr. Grinberg looked at me, his voice choking through his tears, and even in this most emotional moment took time to introduce me: "my wife, my son."

I hurriedly shook his wife and son's hands, and went to the door. "I am so happy for you." I could barely get the words out, my voice faltering as the tears poured down my cheeks.

Dr. Grinberg nodded his head in sudden jerks. As I closed the door behind me I could hear the laughing sounds of Dr. Grinberg's voice, then of his wife's voice, then his son's.

Chapter 7 ~

## THE CONFERENCE

Almost two months had passed since its beginning in May, and the hospital at St. Ottilien had not yet received any official help of any kind, either from the army, the military government, or any of the international, American or Jewish relief agencies that were collecting large sums of money from governments, businesses and individuals to help the displaced persons of Europe.

By this time almost all of the patients at the hospital were Jews. They were reduced to the pitiful state of having to go to the Germans to beg for food. The MG had put the distribution of food into the hands of the local authorities. Few Bürgermeisters were about to give anything to the refugees, and certainly not to Jews. I wondered how many Germans gloated, knowing that while they, the victimizers who lost the war, received regular food rations, the Jews who had been their persecuted victims all these years continued to starve under the jurisdiction of their supposed liberators, the victorious Americans.

While we knew that in many individual cities and towns the local military government officers were to blame, we also knew that conditions could have been significantly different had those in higher commands ordered it to be. General George S. Patton, initially in charge of the American zone of Germany, appeared to do little to either punish the Germans or to rehabilitate their victims. In later years some historians would explain this by suggesting that Patton was so anti-communist that he was eager to help Germany rebuild its strength as a continuing enemy of the Soviet Union, even at the expense of the victims of its Nazi era. Some critics have suggested that a degree of anti-Semitism may have contributed to Patton's reported anger with and hostility to displaced persons, including camp survivors, who remained in Germany after the war. General Eisenhower, in Paris, had more than once stated that the surviving Jews in Germany should get special treatment. It appeared at the time, however, that Eisenhower did little, if anything, to be sure that his orders were enforced.

Whenever I saw Dr. Grinberg during those months he seemed more and more depressed. "The people here have lost hope," he told me one day. "We thought we would at least receive the necessities of life from the Americans, but it seems our destiny is to be deprived of them now, just as we were before and during the war."

While two months may not seem long in a normal existence, it can be interminable to sick, starving, dying people. Finally, Dr. Grinberg's letters to relief organizations began to get attention. The United Nations Relief and Rehabilitation Association (UNRRA) sent a group to investigate the conditions and needs at St. Ottilien. Six or seven UNRRA representatives stayed in the area for a full week. I met several of them one day when I visited St. Ottilien.

They examined the situation minutely: the living conditions, the medical resources and care, the food needs and availability, the scarcity of clothing. They talked with dozens of patients, ascertaining their psychological as well as physical needs. Before they left they guaranteed Dr. Grinberg that help would be on the way. Help did come: six months later, in January 1946, when the worst was already over. Perhaps to compensate for its better-late-than-never behavior, the UNRRA team that finally came, unit 531, not only provided needed supplies, but helped the survivors who still remained at St. Ottilien complete the arrangements necessary to join relatives they had located in other countries.

Better late than never? Not for those who died because of the lack of food and medicine between the initial UNRRA visit and the time unit 531 finally arrived. For them, it was never.

Following the disappointment of UNRRA's first unproductive visit, hope was rekindled on July 15, 1945, when a group of five men representing the Joint Distribution Committee (JDC), a U.S. private relief organization funded to help the survivors in Europe, came to St. Ottilien. Their leader was a Dr. Rock, who told Dr. Grinberg that they had come to St. Ottilien to visit and "to see the children." Dr. Rock was accompanied by a Mr. Halzer and a Dr. Hyton. After several days, Rock advised Dr. Grinberg that the JDC wanted to help St. Ottilien. It seemed that Rock's promise would be kept when, shortly afterwards, Harold Trobe, the JDC's field representative for Europe, arrived. However, he brought no assistance but only the excuse that the JDC could not provide help because it was allegedly being restricted by the U.S. military authorities. But he gave no explanation of what restrictions had been placed on the JDC or why.

Still another JDC representative, a Dr. Pearl from the office in France, came to St. Ottilien. He too investigated conditions at the camp. When he departed, he was more to the point than his predecessors, flatly telling Dr. Grinberg not to expect any help from the JDC. He gave no reasons. The JDC was true to his word. The last time I visited St. Ottilien before my return to the United States in March 1946, Dr. Grinberg informed me that the JDC still had not sent any direct help.

In July, St. Ottilien was officially listed as a displaced persons camp. At first this was welcomed. We assumed that such status would entitle it to at least a minimum ration of supplies and the official aid of the U.S. forces. What actually happened was quite different.

I first found out about the new status on one of our food delivery trips. Soldiers with Military Police (MP) armbands were erecting a fence of barbed wire around the area where the Holocaust survivors were quartered. They were working on the entrance to where the survivors' buildings were, a large gate between two stone and concrete walls. But that part had not yet been completed, and we drove past them and stopped in front of Dr. Grinberg's office, where we carried in our packages of food.

"They are building a fence," Dr. Grinberg explained, "because we are non-persons. Your military headquarters has ordered that all official displaced persons are to be put in guarded camps."

"Why?" I asked.

He didn't know. He had been told that it was to protect the survivors from outside agitators, from angry Germans who might seek further vengeance against the Jews for the continuing shortage of food and shelter in Germany, which had not yet begun its reconstruction. He believed it actually might be to keep the survi-

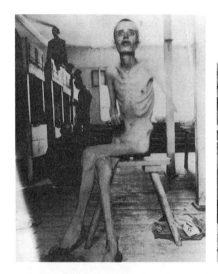

Pictures from Dachau. A few survived . . .

. . . most did not.

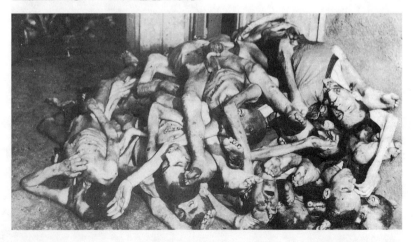

At the St. Ottilien hospital, September, 1945: Monty, 14, second from left, had fought with the Partisans; Shalom, 5, at the right, and the two men, survived Auschwitz.

A Survivor and a child who was born in the woods of Bavaria, at St. Ottilien, September, 1945.

Dr. Zalman Grinberg , head physician at St. Ottilien, September, 1945.

A Committee of Liberated Jews in Bavaria was established in July, 1945.
Dr. Zalman Grinberg is seated third from the left. To his right is Chaplain
Abraham Klausner. FROM THE MINTZER COLLECTION, MAGNES MUSEUM

At the Kaufbeuren Air Base, July 1945: some of the GIs who helped St. Ottilien
(l. to r.): Al Bergman, Ernie Belkin, Edward Herman, and the author.

In his *Memoirs,* Elie Wiesel states that "de-Nazification wasn't really serious." For months after the end of the war, under the American occupation in Bavaria, posters like these were still seen on walls in some schoolhouses, factories, and office buildings.

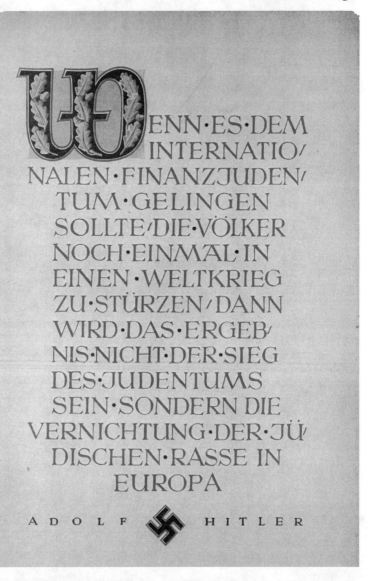

WENN·ES·DEM
INTERNATIO/
NALEN·FINANZJUDEN/
TUM·GELINGEN
SOLLTE/DIE·VÖLKER
NOCH·EINMAL·IN
EINEN·WELTKRIEG
ZU·STÜRZEN/DANN
WIRD·DAS·ERGEB/
NIS·NICHT·DER·SIEG
DES·JUDENTUMS
SEIN·SONDERN·DIE
VERNICHTUNG·DER·JÜ/
DISCHEN·RASSE·IN
EUROPA

ADOLF HITLER

"Should the financial conspiracy of international Jewry succeed once again to drive the people of the world to war, the result will not be victory for the Jews, but the destruction of the Jewish race in Europe. —Adolf Hitler" (September, 1941)

"The freedom of our people comes before the freedom of the individual. —Adolf Hitler" (August, 1939)

There is no alternative but to win, and we will win! —Adolf Hitler" (August 1940)

"National Socialism is the highest expression of the military man in life. —Hermann Göring" (January, 1940)

DER
FÜHRER
HAT
IMMER
RECHT

WOCHENSPRUCH DER NSDAP. / HERAUSGEBER REICHSPROPAGANDALEITUNG / FOLGE 8, 16. – 22. 2. 1941
ZENTRALVERLAG DER NSDAP., MÜNCHEN

"The Führer is always right." February, 1941

The author in front of the 2nd Air Disarmament Wing
Headquarters at the Kaufbeuren Air Base, September, 1945.

The author (l.) and his
associate editor of the *2nd
Wing Eagle*, Anthony
"Dee" DiBiase, in their
newspaper office at the
Kaufbeuren Air Base,
September, 1945.

## THE WORLD

# Euthanasia After U. S. Moved In

### By VICTOR H. BERNSTEIN
*Staff Correspondent*
*(Copyright, 1945, by The Newspaper PM, Inc.)*

 MUNICH, July 5.—German personnel of the Kaufbeuren Sanitorium and Insane Asylum, about 30 miles south of here, were still killing children by injections a full month after the Americans had occupied this town, it was revealed today.

The institution is within rifle shot of the Military Government headquarters and the offices of the CIC—Counter-Intelligence Corps—of the local area, yet no steps were taken to stop these killings.

What makes the situation worse is that there is indisputable proof that certain American military authorities were apprised of what was happening in the asylum as long ago as June 19, and again nothing was done except to arrest certain asylum officials on purely political grounds—because these particular officials happened to be Nazi Party officers of a rank subjecting them to automatic apprehension.

One reason for the lack of action was that there was no doctor attached to the local military government.

It was not until Maj. Marvin Linick, of New York, chief health officer for the Munich Military Government, and his assistant, Capt. Loyal W. Murphy, Memphis, Tenn., moved into the picture a few days ago that the full story of what has been happening at the asylum was made known and steps were taken to arrest the guilty—whether they were party members or not.

Maj. Linick's investigators found that the last child was killed by injections at Kaufbeuren on May 29—21 days after VE Day and 31 days after American forces moved into the town. Moreover, Maj. Linick's investigators found in the non-refrigerated morgue of the hospital the bodies of nine adult inmates who had died from starvation not more than two or three days before. The lightest of these corpses weighed 54 pounds; the heaviest weighed 66 pounds.

(According to a BBC broadcast, picked up by NBC, officials of the murder factory insisted that they continued their "experiments" after the armistice and American occupation on order of "certain German civil authorities" whose names they would not specify. They protested that they were performing experiments "for the improvement of the race." Many cripples and deformed children were among the murdered inmates.)

### Records Also Cremated

The Kaufbeuren asylum belongs to the same network of "mercy killings" institutions as the asylum at Haar-Egelfing which I described in these columns on June 30. Like Haar-Egelfing, it operated under the specialification of the Reichs Committee for Serious Hereditary Diseases and Malformations in Berlin.

And again, like Haar-Egelfing, children and adults were killed both by drug injections and starvation.

Nurse Woerle, an employe at Kaufbeuren, has confessed to Capt. Murphy that she killed at least "211 minors" in the last two years—and that she got 35 reichsmarks—about $14 at normal exchange rates—a month bonus for her work.

Nurse Woerle closed her verbal testimony by asking plaintively, "Will anybody do anything to me?"

It is impossible to estimate how many have been killed by drugs and starvation at Kaufbeuren since the murder routine started in 1940. Many records were destroyed, but on a basis of partial records which have been recovered, there are definitive entries showing that 26 inmates were drugged to death this year up to May 29; 75 in 1944 and more than 60 in 1943.

There are no adequate records to show how many inmates were starved to death. The bodies were cremated on the grounds and apparently at the same time the telltale records were shoved in with the bodies.

Another example of the U.S. Military Government's genocide by neglect: This page from the July 5, 1945 edition of the New York newspaper *PM*, tells how the MG took no action to stop the continuing murder of children in the "children's hospital" in Kaufbeuren for a full month after U.S. forces occupied the city.

Records available do show that the death rate at the asylum, which had a total capacity of about 300 inmates, rose from 4.6 per cent in 1939 to 25.6 per cent in 1944.

Moreover, the killings at the hospital were apparently well known to the inhabitants of the town of Kaufbeuren, which is the capital of the Swabian District and has a population of about 13,000.

One child on the streets of the town, chosen at random, was asked about the asylum buildings and he said, "Oh, that's where they kill them." And a nurse at the asylum, commenting on records which showed that many inmates were shifted from Kaufbeuren to Haar-Egelfing, Linz, Gunzburg and other towns where similar institutions were located, said to the American investigators:

"Some of the people in town objected to the smell of burned bodies in our crematorium. So we sent some of our inmates elsewhere to be destroyed."

Since I wrote the Haar-Egelfing story and learned about Kaufbeuren. I have been asking Germans in Munich whether they knew that inmates of German asylums were being killed as a regular matter. Most say they knew. But they insist they didn't know that many were killed by slow, torturous starvation.

## Letters Prove Brutality

All to whom I talked insisted they thought only that "hopeless cases" were killed and then only by quick humane means.

But the letters found at Kaufbeuren, on official stationery, dispel forever such a fantastic notion. One example is a letter written in the office of the Swabian State Welfare Assn. to the Director of the Kaufbeuren institution, which reads in part:

"I have the honor to inform you that all patients transferred from your institution on Aug. 11, 1940, have died in the month of January at the institutions of Grafeneck, Bernberg, Sonnestein and Hartheim."

Another revealing letter, this one from the Bavarian minister of health to the chief of the institution at Gunzburg:

"In your letter dated Nov. 13, 1942, you have requested the dispatch to you of suitable epileptics for the further carrying through of your research work. I have had the opportunity to discuss this matter with Dr. Faltelhauser, chief of the Kaufbeuren asylum, and Dr. Pfannmuller, chief of Haar-Egelfing.

"Both are most agreeable to turning over to you suitable stock. For various reasons, primarily patients of Kaufbeuren are to be selected. If that institution does not have suitable material, I am satisfied if patients from Haar-Egelfing are transferred to Gunzburg for your research purpose (*forschungs Zwecke*)."

This letter was signed by Dr. Gaum, deputy in the Bavarian health ministry.

## The Sinister Dr. Conti

The Kaufbeuren records also revealed to me for the first time in an official form the role played by a man of whom I have been hearing for several months but whose identity I never could exactly place.

He is Dr. Leonardo Conti, whose long list of titles include that of SS Obergruppenfuehrer, Prussian State Councillor, Reich Public Health Chief, Chief of the Reich Medical Assn. and Leader of National Socialist Headquarters for Public Health.

The Kaufbeuren records now show that Dr. Conti was the sinister designer of the "mercy killing" program throughout the Reich and the Reichs Committee—known as RA for *Reichsauschuss*—whose stamp always appears on death warrants for children, was his principal instrument.

It goes without saying that all personnel of Kaufbeuren involved directly or indirectly in the killing are now under arrest—and steps are being taken to discover why local American authorities of the town failed to move against those murderers in the personnel who didn't happen to hold Nazi Party cards.

The sisters, Miriam (l.)
and Adele (r.), with Katie
(kneeling) and a GI
co-worker at the PX,
Oberpfaffenhofen Air
Base, November, 1945.

Leonard and Edward
Herman, while in the
U.S. military, meeting in
France in April, 1945.

After Truman ordered Eisenhower to change U.S. policy toward the survivors and the packages started arriving from the U.S. in October, 1945, the patients at St. Ottilien received adequate food and could be treated with appropriate medicines. Shortly after this picture was taken, new clothing replaced most of the concentration camp uniforms that were still being worn.

By the spring of 1946, the children at St. Ottilien had acquired decent cloth-ing and were preparing to emigrate to Palestine.

The entrance to the hospital buildings at St. Ottilien in 1977. It had not changed from 1945.

By 1991 the hospital site and hospital buildings at St. Ottilien had been renovated and the entrance gate removed.

vors from going into the towns to seek food and clothing in competition with the Germans. He had also heard that the military government was concerned that many of the survivors, who continued to suffer from contagious diseases—which the MG had not yet provided medicine or medical supplies to fight—might infect the German populace if they were allowed to move about freely. Dr. Grinberg believed that any such danger was being exaggerated, that he would be medically derelict if he allowed any of his patients with contagious diseases to leave the hospital.

When Ed Herman and I discussed this as a reason for putting the survivors behind barbed wire, we couldn't help but wonder at the MG's special efforts to protect the health of the former oppressors while it appeared to do nothing to assure the health of the victims. Had we talked about such a situation several years after the war, we would have concluded that the survivors at St. Ottilien had been placed in a "Catch-22."

"So they are erecting a barbed wire fence around us," Dr. Grinberg said. "Another concentration camp. An American one."

I forget who was driving the day they started building the fence, but I think it was one of the guys who had been in eeseepeesee. "What the fuck are they building, an eeseepeesee in Germany?" he said when he saw the barbed wire. When we had delivered the food and were leaving, he deliberately gunned the motor as we passed the open gate, sending a cloud of smoke toward the MPs guarding the entrance. "I hope the exhaust goes right up their asses," he said. He gunned the motor again as we started up the road. "Up your asses," he stuck his head out the window and shouted back toward the MPs, as soon as we were too far away for them to do anything about it . "Up your a-a-a-s-s-s-e-s, you cocksuckers!" he yelled. I don't know if the MPs heard him or not, but it gave us a good feeling that lasted all the way back to Kaufbeuren.

Among the orders issued to the MPs who were now in charge of the various D.P. camps was not to allow any unapproved goods to be brought in. That included food. In fact, the very next time we came we were stopped at the gate by the MPs, who confiscated the food they found in the car.

We arranged with Dr. Grinberg a way to smuggle food in. A room on the first floor of one of the buildings that looked like it had been used as a gymnasium or exercise room had been converted into a makeshift synagogue. An ark was constructed into a wall at the front of the room, and from somewhere they had obtained a Torah. Services were held on Friday evenings and on Saturdays. That gave us our opportunity. Every couple of weeks several of us would drive to St. Ottilien ostensibly to attend the services. Some of us weren't even Jewish, and of those of us who were, very few were religious. But we knew that the MPs, in the proper American tradition of respect for religion, would not stop us from attending religious services. Under our jackets and in our pockets, and when the weather began to be a bit cooler, under our overcoats, we would hide as much food as we could.

The MPs let us drive through the front gate, and we would park toward the farthest building, about a hundred yards ahead, at the right of an open area by the side of the building where Dr. Grinberg's office was. As soon as we parked, Tito and the other children in the camp would run up. Their "Hello, Joe," "Got any gum, Joe?" drew no suspicious looks from the MPs. As we handed them gum and candy we also handed each one as much smuggled food as their small arms could carry, and they quickly disappeared around the corner of the building with the food. We were far enough away and at an angle from the MPs that they couldn't see what we were doing. If any of them saw or suspected, he did nothing about it.

As bad as things were for St. Ottilien, they almost got worse. The survivors almost got evicted from their hospital quarters. They had been at St. Ottilien for two months, and the priests in charge of the church complex were unhappy. They had hoped that the occupation of the four buildings would be temporary, and they expected that the occupation powers would provide a special facility for the ill and infirm ex-prisoners. The hospital at St. Ottilien had already turned out more than five hundred people it had nursed back to health, and more arrived daily. It now had a population of some eight hundred. It looked to the priests like they would have Jews in their complex for an indefinite period. A move grew within the church complex to "get rid of the Jews."

The church officials went to Captain Colle of the Landsberg military government and asked for the return of their buildings. Colle was fully cooperative and told Dr. Grinberg that his staff and all his patients would have to leave. The hospital in turn appealed to the region's military government headquarters in Munich, and Colle was prevented from going ahead with his directive. Instead, Colle tried to take away two of the four buildings. This would have resulted in an overcrowding that would in effect halt the hospital's work. Dr. Grinberg found two sympathetic officers in the Landsberg

MG, Captain Trott and Lieutenant Friedland, who succeeding in stopping Colle once again, and subsequently did what they could to provide help. The hospital would stay at St. Ottilien.

Although scores of new survivors came to St. Ottilien for medical care, dozens of others died. Despite Dr. Grinberg's efforts and those of Dr. Katz, who had by then been nursed back to full health, and of several other physicians who now were able to function effectively, the lack of adequate resources was overwhelming.

What could we do? How could we make known the plight of the survivors before it was entirely too late? Certainly, we thought, if the American public knew what was happening, it would want to help. Certainly, we thought, the Jews of America, most of whom had lost family members and friends in the Holocaust, would do what they could to help.

St. Ottilien wasn't alone in its suffering and fear. Similar displaced persons camps throughout Germany and Austria were undergoing similar deprivations.

On July 25, 1945, the first conference of the Jewish survivors of the Holocaust in the American and British occupation zones of Germany took place, at St. Ottilien. I was there. The conference was authorized by the military governments of both occupying powers. The representatives to the conference came from displaced person camps that were, by and large, suffering the same deprivations as St. Ottilien. One of their purposes was to form some sort of organization that through concerted effort might succeed in getting the assistance they all desperately needed. Another purpose was to try to break through the wall of international silence about their plight. They hoped that a joint presentation of their situation would get the press to pay more attention. A third reason to meet was for mutual reinforcement, to share each other's problems and to give each other courage and support in overcoming them. Finally, a most important purpose for many was to try to break the psychological chains of the past few years that still bound them and to establish common goals for the future.

Jewish representatives from displaced persons camps in the Soviet and French zones were also invited, but the former declined on the grounds that they were being treated well and had no need to organize for better conditions. We didn't know if that was true or not. The American military government had cut off communication between us and the Russians following the first heady days of friendship after our joint defeat of Hitler. The survivors in the French zone didn't come, some of the other delegates said, because an anti-Semitic campaign by the French occupation forces had driven almost all of the Jewish D.P.s out of that zone, and those remaining were not able to travel freely.

Despite the urgency of the situation, the conference representatives acted like attendees at conferences from time immemorial. They organized committees and boards and argued over points of procedure and parliamentary rules. Perhaps reentering the normalcy of bureaucratic deliberation was a way of going back into a world from which they had been abruptly torn away. They worked hard, through several days and nights, to prepare documents that outlined the hope for the future of the remaining Jews of Europe.

Representatives from the various camps in the British and American zones of occupied Germany gave short descriptions of the conditions in their respective areas. All recounted much the same experiences. Immediately following their release from living death, there was at first an uncontrollable ecstasy for ex-concentration camp prisoners. In their dreams and hopes for help, they were lulled into false expectation and did little at first to ameliorate their conditions. But they were quickly and rudely awakened to the fact that the improvement of their situations lay solely with themselves, that they would get no help from the outside. They did not shirk this duty. As Dr. Grinberg said at the conference, "we resolved to build our future with our own means."

A future built by people with rights, privileges and material resources could be a worthwhile and lasting one. A future built by people deprived of the necessities of life, hindered by countries that recently tried to destroy them and forsaken by countries that had liberated them, could be only the tragic, hopeless one that so many were now experiencing in the D.P. camps.

One after another these men (I don't recall any women speaking), small and thin and pale in oversized or undersized suits, recounted in sometimes angry, sometimes resigned voices what was happening in their respective camps. The pattern was the same. Even though no official anti-Jewish policy existed, the attitudes and actions of the individual American and British commanders and their units in charge of the camps continued many of the same kinds of experiences the D.P.s had had during the past years under the Germans.

A Mr. Roisen, from the district comprising Salzburg, Austria, told of the trials that faced his group. He declared that the greatest hindrance for his people was the anti-Jewish attitude of the German civilian government, which ruled the area with almost the same powers and control it had held under the Nazis, despite the fact that it was the defeated nation.

This was a theme heard over and over again. It was clear that the military governments of the American and British occupying armies had made little serious effort to change Germany's way of thinking and doing into democratic paths, but had allowed it and the Germans appointed to the high civilian posts to slip back into what appeared to be at least a semblance of the political philosophy and even behavior of National Socialism.

Because the survivors in the Salzburg area were at the mercy of the civilian government, Roisen reported, the food and clothing at the camps were unsatisfactory. The conditions in which they lived, he said, were filthy. They were not even given the wherewithal to keep the camp clean, and an outbreak of disease could have dire consequences.

Roisen also described the conditions at the camp at Mauthausen—the same Mauthausen that had been a Nazi concentration camp—to be identical to those at Salzburg. Mauthausen had the additional problem of having many sick people. The occupation forces provided no doctors, no nurses, no medicine. The only source of aid for the sick was to be taken care of by others at the camp.

The dwellings at Mauthausen, formerly concentration camp barracks, were so poor and crowded that the survivors there pleaded for different housing. The military government arranged for them to move, but when they saw the new quarters, full of insects and lice and worse than where they were, the people refused to go.

This so angered the authorities, Roisen reported, that they abruptly cut off all food rations for the camp. The only food the camp residents were getting was from individual American soldiers in the area.

A Mr. Reichhardt reported on other camps in Austria. "The Jews at Wiis live in terror and starvation," he told the conference. Right after the liberation there were about three thousand Jews in that area, he said, but the mortality rate was very high because of the shortage of food and medicine, a shortage, he stated, that still existed. The survivors complained bitterly to the American authorities, to no avail. Some of the survivors had begun going into the town to try to get some food, by finding it, by stealing it, by any means. This provoked the authorities. The American forces solved the problem by putting an army unit in charge of the camp, which went into the buildings with their guns and attacked some of the dissident ringleaders.

What did it matter? If they were going to die of starvation, they might as well die of beatings, and they continued to protest. In an effort to stop the unrest, the military government finally ordered an allotment of 1,200 calories for each person each day. Even though this was less than each German in the area received, it would be enough to keep them alive. But it turned out that they were actually given only 700 calories per day. What happened to the rest of the food? Most of it went on the black market; some of it was skimmed off the top and given to favored German civilians. The protests continued and one night, Reichhardt recounted, thirty Jews in the camp were arrested and imprisoned without apparent cause or reason until the following morning.

"The reign of terror continued," Reichhardt said. Not by Nazi storm troopers, but by American Military Police. All communication was cut off. Food and clothing were withheld. The only condition under which the Military Police would release the supplies was if the women in the camp had sex with them. The word "rape" was not used in this context then; in retrospect, there is no question that that's exactly what the American soldiers had done to the survivors.

The American Military Police always made a big display of the guns they carried, Reichhardt said. He told of one incident at the camp at Urfell where a survivor was shot by an American soldier who claimed he was just "playing" with his gun.

One has to have a notion of what these survivors had undergone during the war in order to understand the sheer horror of what they were experiencing after the war. The women were the most vulnerable. One woman—I'll call her Tania—told me one day of her life in the concentration camps.

"Shall I tell you what I did for two years in the camps?" she asked me one day. It was a rhetorical question because she knew I had been talking with other survivors about their experiences. "When they killed my husband and child at Birkenau, why do you think they spared me? Because I was young and pretty. Because I could be useful to them. They put me in a room in the camp. In a building with other women. They called it a recreation area for the German soldiers in the camp and the soldiers coming through. For two years, day and night, soldiers came through. I stopped thinking of days or weeks. I stopped seeing the sun or the stars. I just lay on my back for two years, day and night. Can you guess how many

German soldiers over those years? Three thousand? Five thousand? Ten thousand? I don't know. I don't want to figure it out because it is too painful to think back on. At first I was grateful when my menstrual periods came. They let me alone for almost a week. But it gave me time to think and after a while I began to dread that time alone. Do you know how many abortions they gave me over those three years? You could go four or five months before they noticed and then they took you to the hospital. At least three or four abortions. Sometimes when a woman got pregnant they simply killed her. Some of the women died during their abortions. They were lucky."

It was after we had heard the reports of the American MPs raping survivors that Tania said to me, "What's the difference between you Americans and the Germans except that you don't have gas chambers?"

For much of the day the reports went on, the same stories over and over, a growing sense of helplessness. Some places were better than others. In the newly built D.P. camps at Belsen and Buchenwald, for instance, conditions were reported to be at least satisfactory, with adequate food and clothing. Conditions varied at different camps in the American zone. To some degree, the problem of inadequate aid was due to the incompetent administration of the American officials; there appeared to be no clear policy of coordination. The greatest disappointment reported by all of the representatives, however, was the lack of help from the world's Jewish communities. Not one foreign Jewish organization, not even from wealthy America, had come to help them. Not one Jewish organization was present with aid after the liberation of the camps.

I felt a growing sense of anger—anger at my own country, at the army that during the war I had been proud to serve in, in order to defeat Nazism. But was Nazism defeated or was it embraced by the conquering army? After the testimonies were over, the conference ended for the day. I found it difficult to look back at those who stared at me in my U.S. military uniform. I was not responsible for the American actions, but nonetheless I felt a sense of guilt.

At all of the displaced persons camps in Europe with Jewish survivors, regardless of how trying the situation of the moment or how bleak the future, there was one common cry from most of the people that was repeated again and again to any individual or organization who visited the camps: "Let us go to Palestine." Many of the survivors had relatives in the United States, and as soon as they could locate those relatives and as soon the U.S. bureaucracy could get around to arranging for visas and transportation—arrangements that in some cases dragged on for months and even years—they would emigrate to America. Similarly, some survivors had relatives in England and wanted to go there. But the overwhelming number had no relatives left alive anywhere.

They had learned their lesson. After World War I, during which more than a quarter-million European Jews had been killed, many in pogroms, they thought the end of the war meant the end of tyranny, and that they could have a normal, peaceful life in their native countries. How wrong they were! Now they *knew* it was folly to attempt to return to what had been their homelands. Other countries in Europe were also out of the question for most; these countries had been willing participants in staining the soil of the continent with the blood and ashes of six million Jews. The continuing post-World War II pogroms in much of Europe were convincing evidence.

The only hope for the future, they felt, was in Palestine. The survivors had seen two miracles: that they themselves still lived and that Palestine had survived the war. Roisen reported that of the sixteen thousand Jews then in Austria, about seventy percent were eager and ready to migrate to Palestine. The same was true for the fourteen thousand Jews in Bavaria.

The representatives worked through the night to write a set of resolutions for a future that might not even exist, but that they had to believe would come. I watched and listened as the remnants of five thousand years of a culture presented a new charter to proclaim to the world that they had not been completely extinguished. It was a Bill of Rights for the survivors of the Holocaust.

The preamble read: "The representatives of the Jewish survivors on German and Austrian soil, participants in the conference of St. Ottilien, July 25, 1945, decided upon the following resolutions for the restoration and preservation of the Jewish race in the world."

The fourteen resolutions were:

*I. Jewish State—Equal Member*

The survivors of European Jews who have been annihilated as a people and led toward final extermination, whose sons and daughters fought the common enemy in the forests of Europe as partisans, in the streets and foxholes of the ghettos, in resistance groups of all European countries, in the Allied armies and in the Palestinian volunteer units in the Jewish Brigade claim:

1. Immediate restoration of Eretz-Israel (Palestine) as a Jewish State.

2. Its recognition as an equal member of the United Nations and participation at the peace conference.

*II. Emigration*

Over the graves of seven [sic] million Jews who have been murdered in Europe we are claiming that the gates of Eretz-Israel be immediately opened for the remainder of the Jewish population in Europe, the bulk of whose men and women have been killed in gas chambers and crematoria. The history of the last six years shows that there is no way back to our native countries because its soil is stained with our blood. It is in Eretz-Israel where our wounds will be healed, where in peace and freedom we shall build our new life.

Should the doors or Eretz-Israel continue to be closed, we shall fight for our living rights by all means possible.

*III. Incorporation in the Jewish Brigade*

We claim that the right be granted each young Jewish survivor to enter the fighting Jewish Brigade.

*IV. Unity*

The ex-prisoners of German concentration camps, at their first conference, are addressing the Jews of Palestine to tell them that during the time of horrible existence in the ghettos and concentration camps, in the days of dark disillusion and pessimism as eyewitnesses to the annihilation of our families, our vision of a united population building its peaceful home in Eretz-Israel has not vanished. We claim, therefore, that the youth, the *Yishuv* and the whole Jewish people should do everything in their power to make this vision a reality. Only a united people will be strong enough to face the difficulties that lie ahead on our path to the future.

*V. Appeal to Jewish Youth*

The Jewish survivors on German soil address this sincere appeal to the Jewish youth, to Jewish fighters under allied flags, to the whole Jewish race:

Awaken, Israel!

Love of Israel!

United Israel!

*VI. Jewish Banner and Symbol*

To put an end to the denial of our existence as a people, we claim that in every place where Jews are living, the Jewish banner shall be floating, and that all Jews shall be the bearer of the Jewish symbol.

*VII. Congratulations to Partisans*

We congratulate the Jewish partisans who have fought the common enemy, and we wish to build our Jewish home together with them.

*VIII. Collection of Documents*

The conference puts forth the claim of all Jewish survivors and institutions that:

1. The names of all the murdered people be registered.

2. The traces of Jewish life be conserved for generations to come. To achieve this, then, it is necessary to collect all the documents of cultural and aesthetic value on the European continent dealing with the Jews and bring them to Eretz-Israel.

*IX. Reparations*

Those who survive, as participants in the war, claim full compensation for Jewish property that has been stolen or destroyed, to be framed in German reparations. Such reparations will be used for reconstruction work in our own land.

## X. Criminals of War

We claim for the Jewish people, the group that has suffered the heaviest casualties, the right to have a representative at the international commission for criminals of war, and that Jewish witnesses be present at the trial to depict and make clear to the world in what a horrible way the Jews of Europe have been tortured by the Nazi murderers.

## XI. Invalids' Pension

We claim for every Jew who became an invalid in the concentration camps a lifelong pension because of the acts of Germany.

## XII. Cultural Life

We claim that we shall have an immediate restoration of a productive and cultural life, that schools be opened in technical and agricultural studies, in languages, that reading rooms and libraries be obtained. Teachers shall also be brought from Eretz-Israel for instruction purposes.

## XIII. Searching for Family Members

This conference calls for the immediate organization of central institutions that shall send delegates to all Jewish settlements and whose duty shall be to bring together separated families and to register the names of victims and of those found alive.

## XIV. Regime of Camps

We call for an immediate liquidation of military guards and military discipline in the camps. Inmates of the camps are no longer prisoners, and have the right to live as free and independent people, fairly fed and properly clothed.

It was the last resolution that interested me most at that time. After all, that was my principal involvement with the survivors: to help them continue to survive. I confess I didn't pay too much attention to the resolutions about Palestine, although I understood and believed that there should be some place in the world the survivors could go that they could call home. I guess growing up in the United States in a multicultural society that even in its racism and prejudice permitted people to at least survive in ghettos, something that the Jews in Europe weren't even allowed to do, made it difficult for me to experience the passion and urgency about Palestine. Yet I understood it. Clearly, if the remnants of European Jewry were to survive, they had to do so in a place where they would find acceptance, support and opportunity. That place, in the immediate post-World War II world was, of necessity, Palestine.

Chaplain Abraham Klausner, who had worked so assiduously on behalf of the hospital at St. Ottilien, spoke at the conference. Part of what he said eloquently summed up the continuing problems and needs of the survivors: "We have informed all the Jewish organizations abroad about your camps, but no one came to help us. We must take into consideration the fact that a large number of Jews in Germany at the present time will have to remain here this winter. From what we have seen of relief, there will be no help. UNRRA has promised clothes and shoes. We have received . . . nothing! It seems we must care for ourselves—get our own food— find our own clothing! We have called upon the Jews of the world to help. So far they have failed."

# Chapter 8 ~

## THE CRUELEST MONTH

August 1945, was an especially cruel month for the survivors at St. Ottilien. Enough time had passed that some help should have arrived. The indifference of the Allied governments, of their commanders and, cruelest of all, of the Jews and Jewish organizations in the United States to the plight of the remaining Jews of Europe heightened the oppression of the heat of the days and of the chill of the nights blowing from the not-too-distant Alps.

St. Ottilien wasn't alone. The July 25 conference report prompted continuing examination of what was happening in other areas as well. The Jewish Central Information Office in London, for example, tried to determine the conditions of the survivors in the Russian zone of eastern Germany and in the Allied zones of Berlin. Its findings epitomized the feelings of Jewish survivors almost everywhere in Europe, who, it stated, were "deeply disappointed that liberation has not fulfilled the hopes it had raised . . . [they are mortified by] the indifference shown by the British and American authorities . . . listening for years to expressions of sympathy and promises of help, they were led to believe that the end of Nazism would be followed by immediate relief and rehabilitation . . . unless help arrives quickly, the problem of the Jews in Berlin will be largely solved by suicide and death."

An August 25, 1945, report by the Jewish Central Information Office on the approximately five thousand Jewish survivors in Berlin stressed the need for food, clothing and medical supplies, the release of prewar Jewish funds still held in German banks and the opportunity for jobs. The report noted that unless they were imprisoned for political reasons, the surviving Jews did not qualify for full food rations.*

Individual GIs at the Kaufbeuren air base continued to help as much as possible. Ed Herman and I went frequently to St. Ottilien, each time becoming more depressed and frustrated by our inability to do all that was needed, and more and more angry at both the U.S. military and civilian sectors for their abandonment of the Jews of Europe.

One nearby army unit, the 433rd Medical Collection Company, was providing some unofficial help to St. Ottilien with food, clothing and, especially, some medicine. We wondered if it was just a coincidence that its commanding officer happened to be Jewish.

By mid-August St. Ottilien had seven hundred and fifty patients, eighty percent of whom were without decent clothing or shoes, and all of whom were malnourished because of the lack of proper food, and unable to overcome their illnesses because of the lack of medical supplies. Even so, the urge to live continued and already five babies had been born, even though there were no facilities and no clothing for the newborns. (More than forty years

---

* See appendix for text of this report.

later, after I gave a speech in Sydney, Australia, on St. Ottilien and the continuing struggle of the Jews after liberation, a woman came up to me from the audience and introduced herself. "I was one of the babies born at St. Ottilien," she said. Like many survivors who were kept out of Western countries because of restrictive immigration policies, her parents found an open door in China and migrated to Shanghai, subsequently joining many other survivors who settled in Australia.)

After one of our visits in August, Ed Herman wrote to his parents about the condition of the people at St. Ottilien: ". . . after six years of hell—and torture—they have not yet been liberated."

One early morning I got a message that one of the survivors at St. Ottilien had been shot. Dr. Grinberg had called the newspaper office, wanting our help. I immediately located Ed Herman. "We lousy privates aren't going to have any clout," he said. "We need an officer with us."

We went to the officer's quarters and got Lieutenant Manheim, who requisitioned a jeep. We arrived at St. Ottilien in little more than half an hour. A hundred yards to the right of the gate, on the outside of the barbed wire fence that surrounded the hospital, a man was lying on the ground. Dr. Grinberg and some of the other doctors were around him. A larger group, perhaps a hundred of the hospital residents, pressed along the inside of the fence. A continuous angry muttering was punctuated with occasional sharp shouts. Several American MPs, their guns drawn, stood between the crowd and the man on the ground. As we approached, an MP captain came toward us. Lieutenant Manheim identified himself.

"What happened?" he asked the MP captain. By that time

we were near where Dr. Grinberg and several assistants were treating the man on the ground. He was under a blanket, his right leg
partially propped up on a pillow covered with a piece of torn sheet.
His pants leg was slit all the way up. One of the doctors wiped
away blood that kept gushing across the fleshy part of his thigh and
coagulating around his knee and ankle.

"He was shot while illegally trying to get through the barbed
wire," the MP captain said.

Dr. Grinberg glanced up, saw us and spoke without looking
up again from his patient. "He was not leaving the camp without
permission. He was trying to get back in. He had sneaked out last
night to go to Buchloe to see if he could find some food. We don't
have any food. He was trying to get back in with food for us. They
saw him trying to go under the wire and shot him. Without any
warning."

The MP captain had not let the doctors take the wounded
man into the hospital. "He's bleeding badly," Dr. Grinberg said,
"and he's been out here for over an hour. If we don't get him inside
soon, I'm afraid for his life."

Lieutenant Manheim convinced the captain to let the man
be taken into the hospital.

"How the hell did this happen?" Manheim asked the MP
captain.

"They know they need permission to get in or out of the
camp," the captain answered. "We have our orders and they have
their orders. We're guarding the camp, and one of our guards saw
him trying to get through the fence."

"That man was in a concentration camp. He survived the concentration camps," Manheim said. "How the hell could you let him be shot?"

The captain looked at Manheim without blinking an eye. "He's only a fucking Jew. That's what all Jews deserve!"

For a moment we were shocked, then without a word the three of us turned and walked away. Behind us we could hear the captain muttering about "fucking Jew bastards."

As we walked into the hospital, we wondered aloud whether there was anything we could do about the shooting and about the MP captain. "Couldn't we get him court-martialed?"

Probably not, we agreed. "First of all," Manheim said, "the goddamned army put that barbed wire fence up and put that MP unit here to do just what they did. What would they court-martial him for? For doing his duty? And they certainly wouldn't do anything to him for being an anti-Semitic sonuvabitch." We wouldn't fully grasp the irony behind this comment until later, when German war criminals used the "just doing our duty" defense at the Nuremberg trials.

"Sometimes it seems that most of the people running this army are anti-Semitic sons of bitches," I offered.

"If we try to do anything to him, he'll come out clean," Ed said. "It'll be a waste of our time and energy, which we should use to try to do more for St. Ottilien."

The man who was shot didn't die. But they had to amputate his leg.

One army chaplain summarized the situation in the camps throughout the American zone: "We [the U.S. occupation forces] have turned the Jews and displaced persons into looters and robbers—for food."

In the meantime the population at St. Ottilien continued to grow. Patients who had gotten well enough to return to their former homes were coming back to St. Ottilien in increasing numbers, many of them staying at the hospital until they found other quarters. They were still pariahs, especially in Poland, where Jews who had gone back home in the expectation that they could regain their property and resume some semblance of their former lives were being murdered in cold blood by the Poles, especially in Warsaw, Cracow and Lodz.

There were moments of warmth and satisfaction and tenderness at St. Ottilien too. Ed and I tried to visit at least once a week, bringing with us whatever we could accumulate from the men on the base and whatever Ed could scrounge from the PX and from other not-too-viable sources, like the mess hall. To recreate some semblance of the civilized life they had known before, the people of St. Ottilien had weekly Sabbath services at their makeshift chapel, organized by Rabbi Klausner, and on Sundays, musical concerts. With Klausner's help and that of soldiers in nearby camps, they had managed to obtain a piano, three violins, a set of drums, an accordion, a saxophone and a trumpet, and had several soloists who sang, we thought, quite well.

One Sunday the concert featured Brahms, Mendelssohn and several Yiddish folk songs. The hit of the evening, however, was a satirical number entitled "I Don't Care to Wander," with cynical lyrics mocking UNRRA and the JDC. Under ordinary circumstances it would have been very funny; but for the moment it seemed bittersweet. Nevertheless, it was a good feeling to know that after all they had been through, the survivors could begin to laugh again.

Both the Sabbath services and the concerts were held in the same room, a former gymnasium that remained unheated even after fall arrived. Among other things lacking at St. Ottilien was coal, necessary to feed the furnaces that heated each building individually. At the Saturday services and the concerts, even after many months, many of the people were still in their striped camp uniforms. Some were in torn and patched used clothing. A few were in decent clothes, mostly GI uniforms illegally donated by sympathetic soldiers. And a few had nothing to wear but the discarded uniforms of the hated SS.

We always brought something with us. By mid-August most of the adults who had gotten well had left. Of the seven hundred and fifty survivors at St. Ottilien, almost two hundred were children. We would get as much candy as we could from the PX and from individual soldiers to take to the children. Sometimes Ed would bring cigarettes for the adults. Occasionally we were able to steal oranges from the mess hall; these were a favorite treat for both adults and children.

It was the children who especially tugged at our hearts. Almost all were orphans, with no inkling as to how or where they would live in the post-Holocaust world. St. Ottilien was their only home for the moment and in the foreseeable future.

We always spent time with Tito. Another child we were especially fond of was a five-year-old boy who was called Shalom. His parents were dead. Shalom was extremely bright. He spoke English, Polish, German and Yiddish. But his body was barely there: emaciated, with his legs and arms seeming longer than they were, his face pinched like that of an old man. I remember Ed holding him against his chest as if Shalom were little more than an infant, the boy's thin arms clutched around Ed's neck. As with all the children, the tattooed concentration camp number seemed bigger than it was. Above the number on Shalom's arm the Nazis had added another tattoo, the word "JUDE."

Some of the older children tried to act more independent. Those who were old enough to vividly remember the horror carried it with them, along with the hate they had not only for the Germans but for the world that had let such violence be done to them. Monty was one of these children. He was about 14, and when his parents were killed in a ghetto several years before, he became an instant adult, taking sole responsibility for his own life. He had fought with the partisans in Yugoslavia. He had not been liberated; he had liberated himself. His constant wild, savage stare told us his past and, we were afraid, also his future.

One of the things the survivors at St. Ottilien appreciated most was our letter-writing. Those who had located relatives or friends in other parts of the world—America, England, Australia, Palestine—dictated letters that we translated into English for those who did not know the language, and wrote verbatim for those who knew English but who were too weak to write. We posted most of the letters through army mail, using our own return addresses so we could be sure that the letters reached their destinations, and so that any responses would reach us whereas they might not reach a D.P. camp. What satisfaction and excitement when we received a response and took it to St. Ottilien to read to the recipient.

But most of the time we were frustrated and angry. We felt

we were fighting a losing battle to save the survivors at St. Ottilien. With winter coming soon, it was certain that without adequate food, clothing and medicine many would die. Was there any way we could help prevent that from happening?

Something had to be done, and with the confidence of youth we decided that *we* would do it. But what? About a week later we knew.

# Chapter 9 ~

## The Letter

Several of the guys were in my room, drinking. It was not an idle pastime. For many it was their primary means of entertainment; enlisted men weren't allowed in the officers' club, and privates and Pfc's—which many of us were—weren't allowed in the NCO (noncommissioned officers, corporals and above) club at that time. (Not long afterward a new NCO club was opened to all ranks.) Unless one had a mistress in town or had established a relationship with one of the female D.P.s working at the base—as several of the men had—there was nothing much to do but sit around and listen to AFN (the Armed Forces Network radio station) and drink. The booze was called scotch, although except for a rare occasion when someone, like Ed, treated us to a legitimate bottle obtained while on leave in England or on business in Paris or from the black market, it was usually homemade brew. Sometimes we wondered if its bite came more from denatured alcohol or Kreml Hair Tonic.

There were frequent parties in our room with some of the guys we worked most closely with. Jimmy Holderfield, a ranked professional middleweight boxer whose mission in life seemed to be "booze and babes," managed to indulge in plenty of both. Frankie Kline. Sam Murano, a nice, quiet guy from Pittsburgh who smoked cigars and before we left Kaufbeuren married a D.P. from Holland. Art Campa, one of the few minorities on the base, which maintained the U.S. Armed Forces white-black segregation policy, but allowed some Hispanics to work with Anglo outfits; Art, at five foot six, was the greatest basketball player any of us saw and later played in the professional leagues; had he been a half-foot taller he would have been one of the greatest players of all time. Morris Shapiro, from Brooklyn, who had just received an army scholarship for a six-week course at the London School of Economics with the famed socialist economist Harold Laski.

I didn't drink hard liquor; I didn't even like the taste of beer, although I indulged in both whenever a group got together so I wouldn't feel left out. But I didn't drink much, and more than once I would fall asleep after a drink or two while the party was still going on. Sometimes, after the second water glass of booze, I lay on my bed and felt my eyes closing and my head spinning and I wanted to stay awake because I could hear the laughter at Dee's jokes getting louder and I wanted to join in with the good time and somebody turned on the radio and the Armed Forces Radio midnight music show was playing its theme song, "Out of My Dreams," from the hit Broadway musical that we had heard about even in Europe, *Oklahoma* . . . and the next thing I usually knew I was getting up in the middle of the night to go to the latrine—it was a regular indoor bathroom, but the term latrine carried over from infantry days—and everybody would be gone and Dee would be asleep in his bed, the blanket pulled up over his head.

On one of the drinking nights, I didn't feel like partying and instead went to see Ed Herman. "The only way we're going to get what we need for St. Ottilien," he concluded, "is directly from the States, from the people who would ordinarily contribute to the JDC and HIAS and the other Jewish relief organizations that it looks like aren't going to help."

"That means getting to every synagogue, every YMHA, every B'nai B'rith Golden Chain chapter in the country," I said. "That means setting up a new JDC of our own. How the hell can we do that?"

"We can't. Even if we had enough money and people, we couldn't do it from here anyway."

Maybe we could contact a lot of those groups on our own, we decided. Somebody in the States ought to have a list they can send us. We agreed that we could write to as many people and organizations as possible, telling them the situation at St. Ottilien and asking them to send packages of food, clothing and medicine.

There was one big problem. We couldn't write open letters like that while we were in the army. We could be court-martialed. But there was nothing to prevent us from writing personal letters. We decided to simply address every letter "Dear Friend."

We could send out hundreds, maybe even thousands.

"My brother Lennie is back in the States after a tour with the air force and is traveling around the country," Ed offered. "I think he's involved in War Bond drives. He'll get the letters to important people, people who can get something done."

We realized that it was a lot of work to print hundreds, maybe thousands of letters.

"I've got the printers," I said.

"And I've got the cigarettes," Ed said.

"For a few packs of cigarettes we get the printer who does the newspaper to run off our letters in the middle of the night and nobody will know about it," I suggested.

"And we don't have to mail all of them individually from here," Ed added. "We'll sign the letters and send packages of them to friends in the States who can distribute them from there."

"When do we begin?"

"Right now."

We talked it out, trying to clearly state for ourselves the purpose of the letter, trying to determine the approach we would take, trying to figure out exactly what should go into it.

"We've got to tell them all about St. Ottilien."

"And about the MPs and the military government."

"We've got to make the people back home feel guilty as hell about the people here," I said. "Make them think it could have been them."

"We've got to be sure it creates enough fuss to reach high places," Ed said. "The politicians, maybe even the President."

I said, "We've got to write it so that the newspapers back home will pick it up and give it publicity."

Ed said, "And phrase it so that people don't think we're trying to con them into sending goods that will be sold on the black market. We've got to tell them how and where to send things. To someone whose motives can't be questioned, to someone like . . ."

"The chaplain!" we said simultaneously.

The next day I started writing the letter while Ed talked with the base's Protestant chaplain, Claude Bond. The chaplain was very supportive, Ed reported. "He says to use his name and address as the place to send packages. That takes us off the hook with the colonel and with practically everybody else. How can they come down on us if the chaplain is part of it?"

"And a Protestant chaplain yet. Couldn't be better."

I wrote much of that day. Ed stayed with me, offering suggestions, going over each page as I finished it. By evening we had a letter we were satisfied with. I got the names and addresses of the workers at the printing plant where the *2nd Wing Eagle* was published. Up to that time there had been no news extra or other journalistic emergency that made it necessary to call the printers out after working hours. We got a closed car from the motor pool. We drove slowly through the dark, deserted streets, barely touching the accelerator in order to keep down the noise of the engine; it sputtered like gunfire whenever we speeded up.

A frightened woman greeted us at each printer's house, answering our knock, which echoed excessively loudly in the stillness of the morning, with frantically rushing footsteps, eyes wide with fear peering through the vertical slot of a barely opened door, quivering hands opening it, heads and bodies bowing subserviently to the soldiers' uniforms. The quick explanation to the wives of who we were, to the printers of what we wanted and the packs of cigarettes in Ed's hands turned fright into sighs of relief, then into smiles and finally into eager "*Jawohls.*"

Hours later we returned to the base with some five hundred copies of the letter, bundled into brown paper wrappers, and carried them up to my room.

We opened one of the packets and held one of the letters, swelling with satisfaction, feeling a euphoria of pride. We shook hands and patted each other on the back. "It's beautiful, absolutely beautiful."

This is what we wrote:

*Friends:*

*The Jews of Europe are a dying race. Even now, even after the defeat of Hitler and Nazism, they are slowly being exterminated from the face of the earth.*

*YOU ARE TO BLAME!*

*If you consider yourself a human being, a member of the human race, then you are—although perhaps unwittingly, yet nevertheless certainly—a murderer.*

*For you are carrying out Hitler's plan of destruction of the Jewish race. By your unconcerned neglect, you are just as responsible for the present death of the European Jews as the most diabolical of Nazis was in the past.*

*No, you scream! Well, yes, we scream, as do thousands of Jews in Europe who are today destitute, without food, shelter, clothing or medical aid. We are not accusing you all, for we know that very many of you did not know and still do not know the perilous situation of the Jews in Europe. But we are accusing all of you who did know—all of you who merely shrugged your shoulders and muttered "It's a shame," all of you who have not given and worked and given more to help these unfortunates of a madman's society.*

*We have seen and spoken to hundreds of representative Jews who four months ago were released from the many concentration camps. Jews who thought that the world would look upon them as martyrs returning from the grave and who thought that there was enough justice and kindness in humanity to help them escape from this life of death.*

*But what we have seen and what we have heard proclaims only shame: shame for all those in our world who have not helped—and who at the same time profess to claim a semblance of humanity.*

*These words may be strong—but they are meant to be—for there is nothing too strong or too bitter if it will help prevent the destruction of a human race.*

*We understand that there are many things that you do not know; that you would be only too willing to help if you knew the facts, if you knew the actual situation of the Jewish people in Germany today. That is the purpose of this letter. To let you know what the Jews have suffered, what they are suffering and what you can—and must—do to help.*

*At the hospital of St. Ottilien, near Landsberg, Germany, there are today 750 people, including a staff of doctors. The patients are Jews, attempting to preserve the life they find it hard to believe they still have. The doctors are Jews, doing the best they can, despite the nonexistence of outside aid, to help these people.*

*Four months ago this same hospital was being used to care for German soldiers. At the same time, there were thousands of Jews roaming Germany, sick, tortured, wounded, without food, clothing or help of any kind. One particular group was led by Dr. Zalman Grinberg, former Lithuanian and now head of this hospital at St. Ottilien.*

*For months he has tried to obtain aid for these people. The Germans refused him. The local governments refused him. There were no such things as relief organizations. For these people the Red Cross, UNRRA, the various Hebrew organizations were, although present, nonexistent. The American Military Government would not aid them.*

*It is three months that this hospital has been in operation, and since that time Dr. Grinberg has turned out 1,200 people who have been cured sufficiently enough to leave their sickbeds.*

*But all this has been done without any help from outside, from either the Allied government or from any of the so-called relief agencies of the world.*

*Today there are 750 people in the hospital, all of whom who are receiving one-half the food they need to recover properly, sixty percent of whom are confined to bed because they have no clothing to wear, others who are still wearing their concentration camp uniforms, all of whom are living with lice and disease because of the lack of bed clothing and equipment, and many of whom are not being cared for properly because of the lack of medicine.*

*There have been relief organizations that have visited St. Ottilien: relief organizations that have come without food, clothing or supplies, that have stayed and listened to the tragic story, that have then left and that have not returned or sent any aid whatsoever.*

*The people of St. Ottilien have written for help. We saw a letter sent to the Jewish World Congress in the United States over two months ago. But there has been neither aid nor even a reply. WHY?*

*Perhaps you as an individual would have helped had you known. But you, as the American people, you as the American Jews, have not helped—have refused to help. You, all of you together, are at this moment responsible for the slow continuing destruction of the Jews of Europe!*

*Perhaps you find it hard to believe what we have told you. Perhaps you find it hard to believe what these people have gone through. It is hard to believe because it is so tragic as to be unbelievable. In the next few pages you will find a speech given by Dr. Grinberg on May 27 of this year at what was called a liberation concert, a liberation concert at which the liberated people were too weak to stand, at which the liberated people still could not believe they were free.*

*Read this speech. Read it carefully. Put yourself into the position of the Jews you will read about. Every one of us knows that it could have been us.*

*Read it carefully—and THINK!*

Here we inserted the full text of Dr. Grinberg's speech, which he translated from the German original into English for us to be sure that what we sent was true and accurate. Following the speech, the letter continued:

*Think! It could have been YOU!*

*Are there tears in your eyes? Perhaps? Is your heart full of pity? Probably! Do you feel ashamed and sorry? Certainly! But tears and pity and shame will not help. These people who you have just read about, these human beings who literally have been in hell, who have no more than a vestige of life left, these Jews of Europe still need help, and they need it immediately.*

*We cannot reemphasize enough the tragedy of these people, the slow death they face unless you will help them. For if you let the Jews in Europe die, you are tightening the noose around the neck of the Jewish population of the world. Yes, those of you who are Jewish, you are destroying yourselves.*

*These people need food; they need wines to enrich the blood of the sick, they need fruit juices, they need wholesome foods, they need rich foods. These people need clothes; they need pants and shirts and dresses. If they are to survive the coming winter, they need protection against the cold. They need shoes. The children, even the adults, are walking about without covering for their feet. They need sheets and blankets if they are to combat the lice and the disease.*

*These people need soap and they need medical supplies and they need everything that you have and that you can get. They need the necessities of life, and they are depending on you to get it for them. The intolerable situation of the Jew having to beg the German for food exists. And you alone can rectify that situation.*

*And it is not only this one hospital that we must help. There are dozens of survivor camps where the inhabitants do not even have that which those at the hospital have. Where conditions are a hundred times worse—and where there is also no help.*

*We are not writing to you as lecturers. We are not writing to you to entertain you with a story of tragedy and shame. We are writing to you as members of the human race!*

*We are writing this to you as an appeal—for you are the only ones who can help—and you are the ones who must help.*

*These surviving Jews of Europe want to live. The fact that five children have already been born at St. Ottilien is proof enough. And the Jewish survivors can live if you will help them. We say they will live. WHAT DO YOU SAY?*

On a final page in bold type in a lined box, we wrote: *In view of the fact that the people at St. Ottilien Hospital are displaced persons in Germany, they are not permitted to receive mail or packages.*

*Therefore, the Chaplain of the Kaufbeuren, Germany, Air Base has consented to receive and deliver to the hospital the supplies you are going to send.*

And then we signed our names, and below them, in large type, Chaplain Bond's APO address.

We mailed them out by the hundreds. To wives, friends, fathers, mothers, brothers, sisters and neighbors, to synagogues, clubs, organizations, fraternities and sororities, to Jewish community groups, to YMHAs and YWHAs, to everybody and anybody who might care enough to send a package, to organize support within their organization, to contact a senator or congressman or any other politician who might by conscience or constituent pressure be goaded into asking questions and getting action. Especially, we sent bundles of letters to Ed's brother, Leonard Herman, who made it his personal crusade to let America know what was happening to the concentration camp survivors in U.S.-occupied Germany.

A lot of GIs cooperated in packing, addressing and mailing the letters. In a week we had sent out the initial batch and arranged to get more printed. "Any more names? Who's got more names? Don't forget anybody."

As I recall, army regulations prohibited the mailing of packages from the States over seventy pounds without the specific request of the base commander or the base chaplain. Chaplain Bond had prepared dozens of typewritten slips of paper with such a request and had personally signed each one, and we enclosed them in letters going to organizations.

In the enthusiasm and excitement of sending out the letters, we began to think of the problem as already solved, as if the food and clothing and medicine for the patients of St. Ottilien were already on the way. We didn't want to think that we might not get any response at all. Ed and I talked about that after we had finished sending out all the letters we intended to for a while: "It could be weeks, maybe months before we begin to get packages from the States," we admitted. "Maybe never."

Our concern was heightened a few days later when we showed

our letter to Captain Klausner. He disapproved. Because Klausner was doing as much to help the survivors as any other person in Germany, we took his criticism seriously. He felt that our accusations were too strong, that the letter might alienate some people rather than obtain their support. At the same time he told us that what we had written was true and that "the world should know."

A few weeks later, after the letter had been distributed throughout the United States, Klausner changed his mind. We had continued to print additional copies, and when we told him that we were sending out more letters, he was fully supportive. Perhaps he realized, as we did, that sometimes the only way to fight tyranny is openly and forcefully.

Captain Klausner, ever the chaplain, did want us to change the request for supplies in the new batch of letters we were sending. He thought that much of the shipping space for food and clothing should be replaced with religious books and articles. We refused.

Chapter 10 ⌐

## St. Ottilien's Kristallnacht

September in Kaufbeuren was unseasonably hot. Unreasonably hot and sticky. Almost every afternoon those of us who were not stuck on a work detail gathered on the grassy lawn near the front gate of the air base, relaxed in the alpine breezes from the south, felt the freshness of approaching fall and anticipated with the change of seasons the excitement of boarding a ship to return home. Already a number of Second Wingers had been rotated back to the States for their discharge. More and more were leaving every week.

While most of the men daydreamed about going home soon, Ed and I had another matter to worry about. The Second Air Disarmament Wing had completed its mission and would be soon closed. Those soldiers, such as Ed and I, who did not yet have enough service points to be eligible for discharge would be transferred to other bases. That time was coming soon. What would happen to the system we had established for bringing supplies to St. Ottilien? "If and when" the packages from the States came, who would organize their delivery to the hospital? Captain Klausner took care of that. One day he introduced us to a Captain I. Jacobson, who had just been assigned to the Kaufbeuren base. Captain Jacobson would follow up what Ed and I had started after we left. And, as it turned out, he did.

Almost a month had gone by since we had sent out the letter and not a single package had yet arrived. It was all the more puzzling because Ed and I had received several letters from the States telling us how people had cried when they read our letter, had reacted with the guilt feelings we had hoped they would have, and how boxes of food, clothing and medicine were immediately put together and mailed to Chaplain Bond, as requested. Not only had individuals sent packages, but organizations such as YMHAs, Orders of the Golden Chain and other Jewish—and non-Jewish—groups had made large shipments. In addition, Ed's brother Leonard had let us know that he had distributed the letters to many parts of the country and that he knew that many packages had been mailed.

Our first thought was that these packages, like so many others mailed to GIs all over the world, had been appropriated at army post offices along the way and the contents sold on the black market. But because there would have been so many packages to this one destination, our air base, and because they were not from individual families to individual servicemen or women but in large part from organizations to an army chaplain, even with some stealing, most should have gotten through.

It seemed as though, for some reason that we couldn't then understand, all shipments addressed to the chaplain at the Second Air Disarmament Wing were being held up at the APO embarkation port in New York. In fact, that's exactly what was happening. But we wouldn't learn about it, and why it was happening, until some time later.

Several of us speculated. Was it Eisenhower? Certainly, our letter made him look bad. Was he trying to make it appear that his orders to take care of the D.P.s were being carried out and that the packages weren't necessary? Some of the guys who had been helping St. Ottilien and were eagerly looking forward to the arrival of the packages as a justification of their efforts were especially bitter. "They've been neglecting the D.P.s," I remember one saying, "and now that we show them up they're going to make sure that they all starve!"

"Maybe if Eisenhower showed some guts and made sure his orders were being carried out, we wouldn't have to worry about the packages," another complained.

Two separate but, as we learned later, related events suggested that something was being done.

On one of our trips to the Munich military government headquarters on behalf of the two Polish sisters, we inadvertently met Captain Klausner escorting a distinguished-looking civilian. He introduced us to Dean Earl G. Harrison of the University of Pennsylvania Law School. We didn't known then that he was President Truman's representative to the Intergovernmental Committee on Refugees.

"Oh, you are the two soldiers who wrote this letter," Harrison said to us, holding in his hand a copy of our letter. "We're looking into it," he said, "we're looking into it." And then he was gone.

We didn't know how or why he had our letter, and we wouldn't find out until later exactly what "looking into it" meant: whether something was being done to help the survivors or whether something was being done to harm our efforts and us personally. A few days later another unexpected occurrence gave further indication that our letter must be having some effect. I was in the Special Services office writing copy for the next edition of the newspaper when one of the guys ran in.

"There's a chicken colonel looking for you," he said. "Got one of those plaster smiles that says he's got something up his ass. I said I would try to find you. Want me to tell him I can't find you?"

"He didn't say what he wanted?"

"Not a word. Just asked where he could find you. Grim-voiced bastard."

"What the hell," I shrugged, getting up from the desk.

"He's waiting outside the main entrance, center door."

I had an idea why he was there even before I saw him. On his left shoulder sleeve he was wearing the SHAEF patch of a gold-handled flaming sword on a black V-shaped shield topped with a red-blue-green-yellow rainbow. I didn't notice any combat ribbons among the decorations over his left breast pocket, but he had a number of gold stripes on the sleeve of his Eisenhower jacket, which meant he had been overseas for a while. I guessed he might have been with Eisenhower during the entire war, perhaps from the early days in Africa. His face was serious, almost angry. I wanted to believe that it was because he was upset at having an assignment he didn't want to perform, but I knew that it must have something to do with the letter.

Unexpectedly, instead of the intimidated inferiority brainwashed into every soldier whenever they came near an officer, I felt a strong sense of self-confidence, almost a euphoria. I acknowledged him with a salute. I was surprisingly at ease.

"General Eisenhower asked me to stop by and see you and Private Herman while I was in the area," he said. "The general wants you and Private Herman to know he appreciates your calling to his attention, through those letters you sent to the States, the plight of some of the D.P.s in some of the camps in Germany." He smiled one of those forced smiles that stays caught in the teeth and looks more like a sneer.

"Thank you, sir. It is kind of the General to go to all that trouble."

"The General is glad to have his men go beyond the call of duty, to have a soldier take an interest in what is going on around him," he continued. "After all, that is why we fought this war."

An interest in what? I thought to myself. Selling GI clothes and cigarettes on the black market, stealing civilian goods, feeding and screwing Nazi women, starving and raping D.P. women? He could at least have added something about democracy or humanity or some such thing.

"Now that the General knows about the problems, he wants you to know that they will be taken care of. It won't be necessary for you to send out any more letters." The smile had disappeared and his voice took on the tone of a command.

I looked him straight in the eye.

"I've checked your records," he said in a friendly tone, but with the condescension that colonels seem of necessity to use with enlisted men. "I'm pleased that you have enough points to be going home soon. I'm sure you're looking forward to seeing your family and going back to college."

He had indeed checked my records.

"Yes, sir. I am."

"Well, the General and I hope you'll be able to do so. We still have commitments throughout the world, and good soldiers like you, who take a special interest as you have in your country's affairs, are needed in places where we still have to keep our guard up. Like the Aleutians up in Alaska."

The sonuvabitch, I thought, and started to grit my teeth and tighten my fists. And then I bit my lip to keep from laughing. The ludicrousness of the situation hit me. The Commanding General of the greatest army in the world, which had just won a world war, sends a colonel to threaten to send a private to the Arctic. Okay, you bastard, I thought, threaten all you want.

With the false bravado of what I felt was an earned arrogance, I smiled.

"Please tell the General . . ." and I carefully emphasized the next word: ". . . sir . . . that I appreciate his kind words and his concern. I'm looking forward to going home and expect to be there in a few months just as soon as my points are reached."

The colonel stared at me for what seemed like a full minute but must have been only a few seconds.

"The letters will stop," the colonel said, more an order than an observation. "You and Private Herman should put your talents to better use and improve your positions in the army." There was no more subtlety in either his voice or his words. "If there are any more letters sent out, you had better put in for ski boots." And then the intended coup de grâce. "And the papers needed for your discharge could get lost."

I waited for him to say something more. But there was no

need to. The general's message had been delivered. The meeting was over. I realized he was waiting for me to salute, and I did so. He saluted back, turned on his heel, then stopped.

"Where is Private Herman," he demanded, half over his shoulder.

"I don't know, sir," I said, truthfully. "I think he's off the base this morning."

"When he returns, tell him I want to see him. This afternoon." Then he left.

I didn't see Ed till later that evening. The colonel did find him that afternoon and had exactly the same conversation with him.

We didn't yet know the real extent to which the letter had made waves, but we figured it must be having some impact, even though not a single package had yet arrived.

"Do you think the bastards can really send us to the Aleutians?" I asked Ed.

"They can do anything they want to us," he answered.

"Even lose our discharge papers?"

"Sure."

"So we must be doing something right!"

Our satisfaction was stronger than our trepidation, and we shook hands in mutual glee. How often do two privates have a chance to frustrate a colonel and a general at the same time!

That night we sent out more letters.

In the meantime, we waited and the survivors at St. Ottilien waited. Dr. Grinberg continued to scrounge for supplies. From time to time he was able to obtain some medicine from sympathetic physicians at nearby army bases, and some clothes and food came periodically from individual soldiers on these bases who had written home about St. Ottilien and got individual packages for the survivors. We continued to smuggle in whatever food we could whenever we could.

A special event in September afforded us a great opportunity to do so. The makeshift chapel at St. Ottilien was being prepared for Yom Kippur services. Leading up to it was a series of prayer services. Although St. Ottilien was surrounded by barbed wire and military police, it was not Nazi barbed wire, and it was not the SS, and the people inside did not wake every morning wondering if it would be their turn that day to go to the gas chambers. It was, therefore, with less apprehension than they had felt for years that they prepared for Rosh Hashanah and Yom Kippur, for the first Jewish New Year ceremony for most of them since before the war. There was even an air of almost festive optimism as they looked forward to September 16, 1945.

Even those people who were not religious joined in, to mark the Day of Atonement not necessarily as the holiest day of the year, but as a time of proclamation of their ethnic heritage and the fact that they, as Jews, remarkably, still lived and were free to hold a celebration, religious or otherwise.

Chairs and benches filled the room on either side of a center aisle, which led from the entrance at the back of the building down to the Torah at the front. Even many of those who were very ill and needed food for sustenance were determined to fast for Yom Kippur. As a show of solidarity, some who had become atheists or agnostics in the godforsaken world of the camps also joined in the day-long fasting and self-evaluation with meditation, making the day a symbol of survival and reassurance for the future. It seemed as if almost everyone at St. Ottilien looked forward to the holiday as going beyond religion alone. It was a benchmark of life, and they all tied their intellectual, emotional and physical well-being to the success of the forthcoming services.

I talked several times with some of the survivors at St. Ottilien about religion. Usually it came up during a discussion of the desire to go to Palestine by those who said they were not religious. "Seeing what a supposed god allowed to happen during these past years, I have to say that if I'm anything, I'm an atheist," more than one person told me.

"Do you go to the services in the chapel here?" I would ask. They would tell me they didn't. I then would ask how they would adjust to a country—Palestine—that already had made it clear it would have a strong religious base. "In your country," they would counter, "is religion very strong where you live?"

I told them that in some neighborhoods it was.

"And do you go to a synagogue?" they would ask.

I admitted that I didn't.

"And you live there okay? Nobody persecutes you because you don't go to a synagogue—or a church?"

"Well, there are a lot of people like me in America. It's a big place, with a lot of different beliefs."

"You know," they would answer, "if enough different people from enough different countries with enough different beliefs go to Palestine, it too can be that kind of place." Then they would add: "I must tell you that right here in St. Ottilien there are a lot of Jews who want to go to Palestine, but who, like me, also are . . ."—most could not openly say the word 'atheists'—". . . non-believers."

We assumed that the MPs guarding the camp would refrain from disturbing a high holy day religious service. The worst bigots are often the most devout in their respect for religious symbols and functions, and attending a religious service becomes a magic password. A number of us concealed food under our jackets and in our pockets and went to the service. Some of us were religious and some weren't. There were even a few non-Jews in the group. However, once we arrived at St. Ottilien the guards stopped us, and it was with some difficulty that we convinced them to let us go inside; we assured them that we were not bringing in any food or other items and that our only purpose was to attend the religious service.

The service was already underway when we entered the chapel, and we found seats where we could, fairly well scattered among the congregation. I located a place near the front, close to where Dr. Grinberg was sitting. We were all given yarmulkes as we entered. They must have been pieced and sewn together by the patients in the hospital over days and maybe even weeks. I wondered where they got the cloth. Several people had makeshift prayer shawls. There obviously was not enough cloth to make more than a few. Three men were on the altar. One was Chaplain Klausner. Another also seemed to be a rabbi. Whether he really was or not I didn't know. The Germans had included rabbis among their top priorities for extinction, and few remained. The third man was in the role of cantor and a hush fell over the room as his voice began the deep mournful cry of the "Kol Nidre," asking God's forgiveness for the shortcomings and broken vows of the previous year.

It seemed as if every person who could get out of bed was there. Almost every seat was taken. At the back of the room were some cots and stretchers with people who were too weak to even sit up. Some of the people still wore the striped pajamas of the concentration camps, almost five months after their liberation, because they were yet unable to obtain other clothing. But some now had other clothes—a pair of army pants, a sports shirt from the PX or a dress made from a curtain or the remnants of a parachute or received as a gift "liberated" from a German house and donated by some GI. There were still some of the same faces from the liberation concert of more than three months earlier—tired, sad, sick and hungry. But now the fear was largely gone. This night, for the first time, there was something more: hope. As the Kol Nidre filled the room there was an audible sigh of relief. The Yom Kippur service really was taking place. They had achieved the milestone that had become an urgent, critical goal during the preceding weeks.

There was no joy. After all, it was the Day of Atonement. But there was something else now: an acceptance of life. For some that was still not desirable. For most it was at least now possible. Whether they were gathered there for celebration of a religious faith or for a statement of political freedom, there was a mutual reinforcement of human existence. If they could freely celebrate Judaism, as they were doing, then perhaps they did not have to fear any longer? Even in the celebration of sadness there was anticipation. For many of the people of St. Ottilien, the Yom Kippur service was an important turning point in their lives.

Suddenly there was a commotion at the rear of the chapel.

We heard the sound of boots kicking open the double doors, and we turned to see the Military Police guard unit rush in. "Every GI out of here," one of them yelled, backed up by other loud, threatening voices. They waved their rifles in front of them, pushed people aside indiscriminately, some of the old and weak falling off their chairs onto the floor. "You were told not to smuggle in food," one of the MPs shouted. "We found food you smuggled in." Those of us who were slow in coming were grabbed by the MPs and forcibly pushed out of the room.

The people of St. Ottilien didn't move. They didn't run. They didn't fight. They didn't yell. They just sat there. The hope they had carried into the chapel was gone, and the glazed looks of resignation and hopelessness that I had first seen at the liberation concert returned.

Suddenly, out of the mass of people, one man screamed: "You Americans are Nazis."

Outside, the MPs lined us up, rifles still in their hands. Fortunately, we had several officers with us, and they simply ordered us to follow them out of the gate and to our vehicles. They didn't want to cause more disturbance to the survivors still in the chapel. We drove back to Kaufbeuren.

The MP unit that broke up the Yom Kippur service was Company L of the 319th Infantry Regiment of the 80th Infantry Division. As an ex-infantryman I somehow thought that these soldiers would have had a special respect for the downtrodden, for those who sought peace and freedom, certainly for those who had been the victims of the Nazism they had fought to conquer.

The next time I was at St. Ottilien I talked about the Yom

Kippur service with one of the survivors who had attended.

"It was a memory of another time," he said. "Seven years ago. I remember the date exactly. November 9, 1938. I was in the synagogue and the Nazis came in with their guns and knocked people down and destroyed the Torah and all the holy objects. They drove the people out of the synagogue. Then they burned it. The same night they broke into our homes and stole our property and went through the city and smashed the windows of every shop they thought was owned by a Jew and looted everything. It was called the Kristallnacht. This time they didn't burn the synagogue."

St. Ottilien now needed more help than ever. Not only material, but psychological. The patients and staff needed an assurance that the smashing of the Yom Kippur service was not a prelude of things to come, similar to what they had known under the Nazis. Some of the GIs who had not been to St. Ottilien before Yom Kippur were now eager to help. They not only smuggled in food but joined others of us in assuring the survivors that not all Americans were like the MPs stationed there and that what happened was not a sign of the future but, hopefully, an end to the past.

In a way the Yom Kippur Kristallnacht was the nadir for St. Ottilien. While the problems of survival were far from solved, some changes began to happen. Dr. Grinberg and others representing the hospital had been making repeated visits to the military government office at Landsberg, asking for food rations. None were forthcoming. On one of their visits their request was heard by a Colonel Tohrn (or perhaps Thorne) of the military government's Agricultural and Food section. On September 17, one day after the Yom Kippur incident, through the efforts of Colonel Tohrn, St.

Ottilien was authorized its first official food rations.

Accounts of the treatment of the survivors behind the barbed wire of the MP-controlled camps throughout Germany and Austria apparently had reached several high government officials. Orders were issued that the symbols of oppression, the barbed wire and the Military Police guards, be removed. For the most part the removal was solely on paper. Some of the camps in the American zone suffered even more in the months to come.

But at St. Ottilien the barbed wire and the Military Police guards were taken away. In a letter dated September 21, 1945, I wrote the following to Leonard Herman: "We took a trip to the hospital today to get the proof you asked for concerning the negligence of the JDC. Not only did we obtain this information [which was enclosed], but we learned of some new developments that cleared up some problems. Dr. Grinberg was informed that there would no longer be an American guard unit posted at the hospital. In a very few days St. Ottilien will have the guard restrictions lifted and will post its own sentries. At about the same time the barbed wire fence will be removed. Second, Dr. Grinberg told us that the military government has issued an order that Jewish D.P.s will not be forced to return to their original country, as other D.P.s are. This order, of course, may be changed at any time, but for the moment the Jews here are safe. Evidently, this sudden liberal attitude on the part of the military authorities means that someone must have finally put a little pressure on the proper persons."

Feldafing was the largest displaced persons camp in Bavaria, with six thousand people. It was at Urfell, near Landsberg. Like the other D.P. camps, it was barricaded with barbed wire and su-

pervised by an American Military Police unit. The survivors were
crowded into small rooms, with from twenty to fifty people to a
room, sleeping on wooden bunks three and four tiers high. Sanita-
tion facilities were virtually nonexistent. Hunger and disease were
rampant. It was hardly different from the barracks conditions they
had known in the German concentration camps.

One evening in October 1945, one of the camp residents crept
through the barbed wire and past the guards and went into
Landsberg to try to find some food for himself and other starving
survivors at the camp. He searched throughout the night and the
next morning tried to sneak back into the camp. A guard saw him
and without warning fired at the man. The survivor was hit and
that afternoon his leg had to be amputated. It was a duplicate of
the incident at St. Ottilien.

Dr. Grinberg learned of the shooting and went to see the captain in charge of the Military Police company, asking that the soldier
who did the shooting at least be reprimanded, as a warning to other
MPs not to either deliberately or carelessly shoot at survivors. Dr.
Grinberg pointed out that the American military had said it would
help, not hurt the concentration camp survivors. The MP captain's
answer was simple, reflecting the attitude and behavior of too many
American officers who were put in control of survivors' camps.

"The American Military Police captain said," Dr. Grinberg
told me, "that it was a shame that so many Americans felt so kindly
toward the Jews as President Truman did."

From the time the Feldafing camp was established in May
1945, the survivors there had protested against the unhealthy, de-
grading and life-threatening conditions under which they were

forced to live, as well as incidents such as the shooting and of rape. The American authorities paid no attention to the protests. It seemed only a matter of time before there would be an explosion. A few months later, in February 1946, it finally happened. In desperation, almost all the people in the camp rose in defiance of the U.S. authority that had imposed such harsh conditions upon them. Noisy protests turned into physical disturbances. The Military Police put down the revolt and arrested and imprisoned a number of the survivors they decided were the ringleaders.

At St. Ottilien, however, with the MP guards withdrawn and the barbed wire taken down, conditions improved. Although another army unit arrived at St. Ottilien in November of 1945, it remained only a short time. This unit, the 413th Collecting Company, under the command of a Captain Gable, was the opposite of the previous St. Ottilien guard: Rather than persecuting the survivors, it showed a sympathetic attitude toward them and made special efforts to help provide food and clothing.

With the Military Police gone, the hospital placed its own guards around the compound as a protection against vandals, thieves and the growing number of "werewolves," gangs of young Nazis who terrorized Jewish survivors, displaced persons and other foreigners, as well as Germans who were known to be anti-Nazi or non-Nazi.

The "werewolves" and their successor Nazi and neo-Nazi groups continued throughout the occupation and afterward, encouraged by the American MG's ambivalent attitude toward individual Nazis; by U.S. support of right-wing political groups such as the Christian Social Union (CSU)—the Bavarian equivalent of the na-

tional Christian Democratic Union (CDU)—against the liberal philosophy of the Social Democratic Union (SDU); and by the USMG's
banning of the German Communist party, which had played a leading role in the anti-Nazi underground during the war. The Social
Democrats, joined by some of the communists who no longer had a
political alternative, were labeled socialist, which in turn was
equated with communist. The support for the conservative CDU
by the United States established a pattern that was to continue for
decades, and a legacy that later led to the growth of gangs of young
neo-Nazi "skinheads" a half-century later.

# Chapter 11 ↝

## Who Won This War, Anyway?

It was mid-October, and the Second Air Disarmament Wing had completed its assignment and was being phased out. Bavaria had been the last stand for the Luftwaffe. It was in the toylike, gingerbread cities of southern Germany that the Germans had tried to hide their last vestiges of air power. The harmless-looking cities and wooded areas had been used to camouflage Luftwaffe equipment and material for a final refuge from the relentless Allied bombings. Now, five months after the end of the war, the airfields had been scraped clean, the material collected and either destroyed or sent back to the States for research and further development, and every factory and laboratory disarmed of war-making equipment. Civilian life in Germany began to resume its normal course as the Second Wing released the factories, other buildings, property and land to the military government, under whose control they were gradually being returned to civilian operation and production.

Only thirty men remained in the Second Wing. The others had already been rotated back to the States. Some of us would stay on the base, reassigned to other units. Others would be sent to different occupation bases in Germany. I did not yet have quite enough service points to be sent home.

It had been two months since we had written our letter, and still not a single package had arrived. Ed Herman and I were depressed and worried. The Second Wing's mission had been fulfilled, but our mission, saving the people at St. Ottilien from the hardships of the coming winter, had not been.

Then came the orders that my assistant editor and roommate, Dee DiBiase, and I were being transferred to another unit, the 44th Air Supply, headquartered at a former military aircraft testing field northeast of Kaufbeuren, the Oberpfaffenhofen air base. Ed Herman, however, was not yet being transferred and expected to remain at Kaufbeuren for at least another few weeks. I was relieved that when—although by that time the word "if" began to dominate our expectations—the packages arrived, Ed would be there. We agreed that as soon as the first shipment came in, Ed would call me at Oberpfaffenhofen so I could arrange to be at St. Ottilien when it was delivered.

I left Kaufbeuren a few days after the colonel's visit of October 5. The Oberpfaffenhofen air base already had a newspaper, with an editor, and I was assigned the job of associate editor. While the position didn't provide the prerogatives I had at Kaufbeuren, it did offer some flexibility. Fortunately, several of the officers who had been helping St. Ottilien or who had endorsed my efforts at St. Ottilien, in particular Lieutenant Jack Manheim and Lieutenant Albert Cusick, were also being transferred to Oberpfaffenhofen. I would have support from them for transportation and passes to go to St. Ottilien when it was necessary.

A number of the D.P.s who were working at the Kaufbeuren base decided to move to Oberpfaffenhofen as well, some because they were guaranteed the continuation of jobs, and some because they had established close liaisons with officers or enlisted men who were being assigned there. Miriam and Adele were among them. Rather than their attempting to find someone new to act on their behalf, if necessary, to help them get to an immigration center for transportation to the U.S. when the time came, I suggested that they join me at the new base. Besides, we had grown very fond of each other.

Oberpfaffenhofen was about nine or ten miles from Munich and though further in distance from St. Ottilien than Kaufbeuren, it was on a main east-west road instead of requiring a number of small connecting roads and it took about the same time to get there, a half-hour or so. Those of us who could pronounce Oberpfaffenhofen practiced saying it by putting it in the company of its sister towns, Unterpfaffenhofen and Pfaffenhofen. A German who worked on the base told us it meant "the priest's house a little closer to the church than the other priest's house."

The base was only a mile or so from the town of Neu Gilching and the larger town of Gilching, These were within the political district of Starnberg, a lovely summer resort city on the Starnberger See where Mad King Ludwig was found drowned during one of his afternoon walks. His doctor who was accompanying him also was mysteriously drowned. There were no public witnesses to what happened, but the political overlords who had lured Ludwig there immediately took over his empire.

Starnberg, not only a resort but the center of commerce for surrounding towns, was the regional headquarters for the military government. The Starnberg MG was like most others. Sometimes it seemed as if the U.S. forces were bent on rehabilitating Nazism and the Nazis as soon as they could. The attitudes of many individual officers toward the survivors and the Nazis was compounded by the U.S. decision to return many of the Bürgermeisters who had served under the Nazis to their old positions in their cities and towns. Although ultimate authority rested with the military government, in too many cases the MG either abdicated its responsibility or through sympathy or bribery cooperated with the former Nazis who were put back in power. That was true in Gilching.

Shortly after the area was secured by the American forces, the MG established a new city council with no Nazis. Herr Sohler, the German political boss of the Starnberger district, protested. "Since 1933," he said, "the city council of Gilching has had one hundred percent Nazi membership, and now with the war over we see the council devoid of active party members. It is only right, therefore, that the council of Gilching have at least one Nazi on its membership roll."

Not only did the MG allow this statement to go unchallenged, but it permitted Sohler to arrange the appointment of Peter Hogner, a leading Nazi of the area during the Hitler years, to the Gilching council. Only continuing strong complaints from anti-Nazis, principally the communists (whose party had not yet been outlawed by the United States occupation forces), some displaced persons and former political prisoners, and some of the Catholic priests and Protestant ministers who had been in prison or house arrest during the war because of their opposition to Nazism, led to his subsequent ouster from the council.

Sohler also nominated and got the MG to reappoint as

Bürgermeister of Gilching one Johann Simon, who had been mayor under the Nazis.

Shortly after V-E Day, General Eisenhower had issued an order to all military commands that recently released concentration camp prisoners and any other Jews who needed shelter should be provided housing, even if it meant forcing Nazis to leave their homes to do so. Where there were no homes available, Jews and displaced persons who needed lodging were to be given any rooms in German homes not being occupied by family members. Simply, it meant that the local government was authorized to temporarily confiscate any unused space in houses owned by Germans and arbitrarily allow D.P.s to live there.

You can imagine the consternation this caused among many Germans. Not only had they lost the war, but now their homes, or parts of them at least, were being commandeered for use by those they perceived as having caused the war, caused their current hardship and who should have been totally annihilated in the gas chambers, anyway.

It appeared, however, that Eisenhower's orders were rarely implemented. When survivors in the vicinity of Gilching heard about this order, they demanded that Simon enforce it. Simon refused, stating that the only circumstance in which any Germans would be forced to leave their homes would be if the houses were directly requisitioned by the American forces. In fact, Simon obtained a number of official army "Off Limits" signs that he gave to known Nazis in the Gilching area so their homes would be safe from American soldiers, survivors and D.P.s. At the same time he warned non-Nazi Germans in the town that if he saw such signs on their houses he would tear them down himself.

The American military government did nothing.

Not long afterward a thousand Germans living in small apartment houses were dispossessed to make room for American military personnel. Dee and I, for example, were quartered in a room on the second floor of a two-family house in Gilching. Simon refused to re-house the displaced Germans in the large homes of former Nazi bigwigs; only the continuing pressure of non-Nazi elements in Gilching resulted in one hundred and four of the families being given rooms in some of these homes.

Under the eyes of the MG, Simon distributed food the same way. When extra or surplus food was made available to Gilching he gave it only to known Nazis. The MG did not object when he put in charge of the city's food rationing committee a woman named Berta Wolfe. Her credentials for the position? Membership in the Nazi Party that dated back to June 1931. Simon took care of available jobs the same way. Priority for the public payroll went to his Nazi relatives. When he ran out of relatives, he hired other "deserving" Nazis. Although many of his appointees were incompetent and his operations often charged with inefficiency, he made no effort to rectify the problems. His reasoning: Since these people had held important jobs for such a long time before the Americans came, why not now?

Even tragedy or near-tragedy did not prompt the USMG to discontinue Nazi control of many German towns and cities. In Gilching, for example, Karl Schmidt, an outspoken anti-Nazi, called the town ambulance one day for his wife, who had started childbirth pains. The hospital was ten miles away, in Herrsching, and the lack of gasoline and auto parts precluded any private transportation. The ambulance service was, of course, under the supervision of one of Simon's Nazi appointees. The ambulance, which usually arrived promptly, did not come. Despite repeated calls by Schmidt—and repeated promises—the ambulance still did not come. After three days Schmidt finally was able to get his wife to the hospital himself. He was told that one more day and the baby—and perhaps his wife—would not have lived.

In February 1946, Simon was elected mayor of Gilching in the first elections authorized by the USMG. During the previous months Simon had established his credentials with the MG by writing several articles concerning the evils perpetrated by Adolf Hitler; for the military government, his words spoke louder than his actions. Sohler still continued as political boss of the area. Both men—and other Nazis throughout occupied Germany—ran under the banner of the Christian Social Union. The CSU became the respectable mantle for former Nazis of Germany. Only in later years did the opposition Democratic Social Union from time to time compete successfully in regional and national German politics.

I got involved in several attempts to enforce the orders concerning the houses and property of Nazis. When Miriam and Adele arrived in Oberpfaffenhofen not long after the Second Wing had set up its headquarters, they needed to find someplace to live. Under the housing orders, they went to Simon to seek quarters. After some pressure on the military government, Simon was ordered to comply, and after a few days he reluctantly assigned them to a room in a house in Neu Gilching, a village within easy walking distance of the air base. This was a house to whose owners Simon had been forced to send an eviction notice two weeks earlier under another decree, Government Law Number 52, issued by Supreme Headquarters for implementation by all lower units, which stated that all persons who were considered war criminals or who were in prison for Nazi activities would have their property forfeited.

The owner of the house, a Dr. Remmler, had reputedly been a high-ranking Nazi and was technically under arrest by the occupation forces. In fact, he had disappeared and could not be found. It was a huge old house, almost a small manor, well back from the road, hidden among trees and bushes, with a large gabled roof of curves and indentations so that the rooms seemed to jut out in several directions. One entered through a short, fat hallway into a large, fat living room with heavy tapestries on the walls and fat overstuffed chairs and sofas with needlepoint fabric filling every spare inch except for several too-tall end tables covered with multicolored satin and fringed lace. It was a house befitting a well-to-do, politically well-placed family of the Third Reich. Besides the large living room, there was a dining room, kitchen and bathroom on the first floor, and on the second floor three bedrooms that were reached along a wide hallway.

One of the bedrooms was occupied by "old man" Freund and his wife. He was a Jew who survived the war because his wife was not Jewish, and now, under a military government order, he had been appointed manager of the property and given quarters there. The rest of the house was occupied by the Remmler family—sans Papa, who was busily evading capture and perhaps trial as a war criminal: Christa Remmler, his wife, Molly Schendell, her daughter by a previous marriage, and Beatrice Lindner, their ward. I had already met Beatrice, or Trixie, as we called her. She and Molly both worked on the base, as secretaries and translators for officers. Both had been well educated. Molly, I think, in a university in England, and Trixie in the United States. Both had perfect command of the English language. Trixie said she had gone to Vassar.

Trixie and Molly were both handsome women, perhaps in their early 30s, slim, blond, high-cheeked. They both dressed well, presumably because their important status during the Hitler era entitled them to good clothes, probably taken from France and other occupied countries. Rumor had it that from the end of the war until the Americans took over the air base at Oberpfaffenhofen they had survived on the resources they had stored up during the war and when those ran out they were not averse to entertaining American officers who came through the area, in exchange for money, food and cigarettes.

For those of us who were still in our teens or early 20s they seemed sophisticated, glamorous and sexy. For the somewhat older officers for whom they worked they were much more than that. It was openly stated around the base that they kept their important jobs by sleeping with their bosses. It was no secret that they had both taken advantage of their positions by trying to persuade their officers that Nazism wasn't as bad as it had been painted, that its actions, including those involving the Jews, were justified, and that the Germans were the Americans' best allies and friends in the postwar anti-communist world.

Trixie worked in an office next to Special Services, where I worked on the newspaper. She had started at the base as personal assistant to one of the higher-ranking officers and, as each officer got tired of her, worked her way down. By then she was assistant to the head of the Military Police, Lieutenant John Parks. When I first met her, she was haughty and proud. Nothing about her suggested that her serving each officer in turn was in any way demeaning.

"I am a soldier," she said. "I am doing my Führer's bidding. I know you disagree with what we believe, but like you, I am doing what I can and must do for my country, just as you do for yours."

She was always willing to discuss candidly her beliefs about Nazism, the Jews and the war, and was not hesitant to argue them openly. But she also had a low frustration level. She couldn't stand being teased. Whenever one of us would respond to her praises of Hitler by singing the song that the Spike Jones band had made popular at the time, "And we heil—pfft—heil—pfft—right in der Führer's face," she would turn red with frustration and scream, "But you don't understand. You just don't understand."

We didn't know it at first, but one more person lived in the Remmler house: Wolfram Schendell, Molly's brother and Dr. Remmler's stepson. Wolfram Schendell had purportedly been recently released from an American prisoner-of-war camp where he had been incarcerated under suspicion of having been in the SS. It was rumored that he had either escaped, had bribed his way out or had been released after filing false affidavits about his Nazi past. The order from the Gilching Bürgermeister required the Remmler family to move in order to release accommodations for Adele and Miriam. But the Remmler family refused. Trixie and Molly enlisted the help of two U.S. officers at the base, Major Richard Scott and Lieutenant John Parks—she worked for the latter allegedly in as well as out of bed—who attempted to get Bürgermeister Simon to recall the eviction order. Simon did. However, Lieutenant Jack Manheim, who had taken a leading role in helping St. Ottilien and in locating Miriam and Adele's parents, spoke to Simon and to Major Scott and Lieutenant Parks, and the order was reversed once again. The Remmler family was ordered out and the sisters authorized to move in. By then there was a third young woman, also working at the base, who needed lodging. Katie was Jewish and a survivor of Buchenwald. She was from the Ukraine and the only member of her family still alive. Miriam and Adele had met her in Kaufbeuren and they had become close friends. Together they came to Oberpfaffenhofen and despite their lack of proficiency in English were given jobs by PX sergeant Sam Weisel. Katie had a strong sense of humor and seemed to relish each moment in which she could find laughter or any kind of joy. After she was liberated from the concentration camp, her principal dedication, it seemed, was to make up for her deprivation of food, and working at American bases she made each mealtime a feast. Each day she added more weight to her barely five-foot height until her round body and wide smile made her seem like a bouncing butterball.

A large garage, or perhaps at one time a large barn, was at the rear of the house, and it was here that the Remmler family put their belongings when they moved, taking with them some of their furnishings, including overstuffed chairs, the overstuffed couch and other favorite items. Part of the family lived there and part got lodgings with friends in the area who sympathized with their plight and their beliefs. The Freunds and the sisters and Katie were about to be left with nothing, despite a further decree, Military Government Law Number 10, issued under the authority of European

theater commander General McNarney, that stated that the property of a war criminal confiscated by the military government was
to go to the Jews, displaced persons and other needy. The Remmler
family, however, obtained an order from MG district headquarters
at Starnberg stating that those occupying the Remmler house must
"release all personal property of Remmler and Schendell as furniture, clothing, typewriter, etc., immediately." The order was issued
by Warrant Officer Donald S. Milner and Pfc. Richard L. Kahn. We
later learned that Wolfram Schendell had developed connections
with the Starnberg MG strong enough to have it contravene higher
orders on his behalf. Nevertheless, the Remmler family was pres-
sured into leaving a minimum of furnishings necessary for those
remaining in the house.

Adele, Miriam and Katie lived in a large room on the second
floor, at the far end of the hall. As I recall, it had a single bed, more
like a cot, at the left, a dresser, a night table and one easy chair in the
center, and a larger bed, somewhat bigger than the usual double size,
at the right. Miriam and Adele slept in the big bed, Katie had the
cot. I met Old Man Freund the first time I visited the girls, bringing
them some food, candy and, especially, American magazines. The
sisters, and now Katie too, were eager to get to America, the latter if
and when she could find an American soldier who would be willing
to enter into a temporary marriage of convenience so she could enter
the U.S. as a war bride. She had no blood relatives in the States, a
requirement for facilitated immigration. They were always excited
about seeing *Life* and *Look* and other magazines' pictures of America
and to hear me talk about what life there was like.

Old Man Freund was right out of Dickens. He was in his

mid-60s and seemed to be all jowls. A big, round, fat, bald head, with a few wisps of black-gray hair combed in separate strands across the top from one ear to the other. His body curved outward from his forehead to his toes and back up again like the contours of a balloon slowly losing air. His face seemed to hang down on all sides; when you looked at him you saw only layers of flesh. You weren't ever quite sure whether his eyes were open, or even where they were.

"Welcome, welcome," he said in English. "I am happy to have the girls here, like my own children." His accent was the same I had heard countless times in New York from the old men and women who decades before had migrated from Germany. He virtually pulled me by the hand into the living room, then put his arms around the girls, who had greeted me at the door, his hands furtively caressing their hair, their shoulders, their backs, all the while huffing and puffing his insistence of how happy he was to have them there.

"I'm an old man," he said. "I'm sixty-five. Old. Old. How happy it is to have young girls in the house."

His wife prepared tea and we sat in the living room. His wife seemed somewhat younger, perhaps in her early or mid-50s. She was stout and her body sagged, but her features retained the memory of what must have been a vibrant, intelligent, adventure-seeking young woman.

Freund gesticulated around the room. "The Remmlers—the Nazis—" he said, "they took the best furniture. They left me junk."

Freund's wife went through an alcove into the kitchen and brought out a tray with six glasses in silver holders and a porcelain teapot covered with a Russian tea cozy.

"My tea glasses," Freund said. "It is practically all I have left. I am only a poor Jew. I would be in the gas chambers except that my wife is a gentile. Everything I had I used as bribes to stay alive, to not be deported. When the war was over, what did I have? Nothing. I was entitled to living space. So I went to your military government and showed them that the Remmlers were very high Nazis." He talked only to me, ignoring the girls as though they wouldn't understand. "Do you know Law Number 52?" he asked me, continuing without waiting for an answer. "I studied it. I went to your military government offices and studied it because I can read English. Law 52 says that all persons who are war criminals or who are in prison for Nazi activities can have their property forfeited." He leaned forward to me, confidentially. "Did you know that Dr. Remmler is a war criminal? They haven't arrested him because they haven't found him yet. But it got me a place to live when they made me manager of his property." He smiled, then laughed, his face buried in a mass of shaking jowls.

He leaned back and spoke only to me again. "Do you know Military Government Law Number 10?" he asked, again without stopping for my response. "It says that all property of a war criminal can be confiscated and go to Jews, displaced persons and other needy. I know this because I studied it at your military government headquarters." Then he leaned even closer to me, his voice even more confidential. "I should have had all the house and all the furniture. But the Remmlers, they went to your military government and got all the furnishings and the use of the big barn outside. I got nothing, just what you see here." His voice moaned and he looked as though he were going to cry.

"I will share everything with these dear girls," he offered. "Of course, there is not much I can share. I have no money. Not a pfennig. No money to even buy food. But I am happy to share this house and whatever I have."

I thanked him for his concern and generosity.

"Of course, I could do more for these dear girls if I had some income. I'm not asking, you understand, I am only mentioning it so that if the girls want to pay me some rent, it would help with expenses."

"Would the rent go to the Remmlers?" I asked.

"No, not to the Nazis."

"That's what I thought. Then it would go directly to you," I concluded.

"No, not to me personally. It would be a sharing of expenses, so to speak."

Although they didn't have to, the girls wanted to pay him some rent. Perhaps, after living their entire adolescence without parents, without the opportunity to be or act or feel like children, without having a father or grandfather, even this man might be, in a way, a substitute parent. They wanted things to be as peaceful as possible and to have as much friendship and goodwill from him as they could.

Freund was pleased. "I have a song for you," he announced. He stood up, his body shaking up and down and from side to side as he tapped from one foot to the other, and sang:

"If you lak-a-me lak I lak-a-you
And we lak-a-both the same
I lak-a-say, this very day

I lak-a-change your name.

Cause I love-a-you

And love-a-you true

And if you love-a-me

One live as two,

Two live as one,

Under the bam-boo tree."

He bowed slightly as his audience applauded. He sat down and turned to me. "You didn't ask me how come I speak such good American. How many Germans have you met who speak such good American? Good English, some of them, but not good American."

"Yes, I noticed that, Herr Freund," I responded with grandiloquence. "How come you speak such good American?"

He smiled proudly. "Because I lived in America. For two years. In New York. From 1902 to 1904. I went there to work, to see about becoming an American. But it was hard. The jobs I could get were hard, the hours were long, the pay little. So I knew I wasn't going to become a millionaire in a few years, and I came back home. That song, it was my favorite in America. They played it everywhere. Do you know it? Do they still play it?" He started again, waving his hands back and forth to the rhythm, "If you lak-a-me lak I lak-a-you . . ."

The Remmler house was a comfortable place for the girls, only about a fifteen-minute walk to the Oberpfaffenhofen Air Base, where all three had jobs. Freund had a son, Richard, who was then 29 years old. I got to know Richard well. He was married, and had been to dental school before the war. I never did find out exactly how they had been able to survive in Hitler's Germany. Perhaps it was, as Old Man Freund said, because his wife was a non-Jew? Perhaps it was because, as Freund also suggested, they had been able to bribe the right local officials at the right time? Some others who were Jewish or half-Jewish and survived the Nazi regime had not been sent to the concentration camps for those reasons.

Now that the war was over Richard was completing his dental apprenticeship and had begun a preliminary practice. Both Dee and I, unhappy with the stories we had heard about the base dentist, went to Richard for some dental work. He was good, relatively painless and appreciated the Dienst Marks (DM, the occupation-authorized currency) we gave him for the work. We liked him immediately and it wasn't long before we became good friends.

It was Richard who told me that Wolfram Schendell had been in the SS. A military government order required all Germans who had been prisoners of war by the Americans or who were suspected of being active Nazis and were incarcerated right after the war, to fill out a *Fragebogen*, a questionnaire, upon their release. The *Fragebogen* was given to all German civilians, requiring that they state what their Nazi affiliations, if any, had been. If they stated that they had not been members of the Nazi party and it was later found that they had been, they would be obliged to serve jail sentences equal to the number of years they had been in the party and denied it. If they denied they had been in one of Hitler's elite corps, such as the SS, and it was discovered that they had been, the same penalty applied. For those who had been caught, the average term then ranged from two to five years.

Knowing Schendell's background, several Gilching residents were surprised at his early release. They investigated and, as Richard Freund told me, found that he had lied on his *Fragebogen*. They reported this to the constable of Gilching, a man named Moser. Moser was considered to be conscientious about his job, not known to be a Nazi, and it was believed that he would take appropriate action. However, no action was taken against Schendell. Whether Moser reported Schendell's presence and alleged violation of the *Fragebogen* requirement to the proper authorities, I do not know. But in light of a subsequent incident involving Schendell and the complicity of USMG authorities in trying to hide it, it is likely that Moser did report Schendell and, as in the case of many Nazis in immediate postwar Germany, the MG had a blind eye and a deaf ear, reinforcing for the German people their belief that the U.S. had little serious intention of either de-Nazifying Germany or re-educating the public away from Nazism. If anything, many Germans began to believe that the U.S. was, in effect, telling them that what they had done and believed in for the past dozen years wasn't so bad, after all.

Wolfram Schendell continued to remove furniture and furnishings from the house. One day the girls came back from work and found that their room had been broken into and not only some furnishings, but also some of their personal property, including money, had been taken. The sisters told me about it that evening, and in the morning I confronted Schendell in the barn, which had been fixed up into living quarters. He denied taking any of the girls' personal property. He wasn't to be bluffed and ordered me out of his "home." The theft was reported to Constable Moser, who investigated and found some of the stolen articles in Schendell's living quarters.

Moser sent in a report of Schendell's crime to MG headquarters in Starnberg. Because there was no jail in Gilching or any of the other nearby small towns, it was the practice of the MG in Starnberg to send American Military Police or German deputized police to capture and imprison in Starnberg known criminals or lawbreakers from the towns under its jurisdiction. Schendell's crime was unlawful entry and robbery. Weeks passed and nothing happened. Moser returned the items he had recovered, but others were still missing. Although Miriam and Adele and Katie did not want to exacerbate the situation and wanted to avoid any further trouble, I was furious. They had little enough, their few personal belongings the more precious because of their loss of everything else—home, family and youth, as well as all their material possessions. I drove to the MG office in Starnberg, where I told the officer in charge that day of my concerns. I said simply that I was a good soldier who had learned of this violation of MG regulations and came to report it so that the MG could take appropriate action. The officer, a captain, didn't question my allegations. I had the feeling that he already knew about the case. He jotted down a few notes, thanked me, shook hands and told me he would take care of the situation immediately.

I had driven a few hundred yards from his office when I realized that I had forgotten to give him the complete list of stolen articles. I turned the jeep around at the next block and was pulling up to the MG building when a man got out of a German sports car—it could have been a Mercedes, I didn't notice the make—and went inside. It was Wolfram Schendell. How did he get the fancy car? I wondered. And what was he doing at MG headquarters? I thought it was a good thing that I had seen the MG captain first. I speculated that Schendell probably concocted some story about the robbery that absolved him and came to clear himself. The office was on the second floor of the building and I hurried up the stairs, thinking that I would confront Schendell in the presence of the officer. Schendell had already entered the captain's office when I reached the top steps. The door was open and before I could cross the hallway into the office, I saw the captain get up from behind his desk and extend his hand to greet Schendell.

I stayed out of sight on the landing and tried to listen. Their warm, animated conversation made it clear that they were friends. They spoke first about automobiles and how Schendell had access to the best cars in the area. He had brought this one, as previously arranged, for the captain's personal use. They talked briefly about women and then about a particular woman. It sounded like Schendell had been able to procure one for the captain, to go with the car. The captain thanked Schendell for both. He offered to have someone drive Schendell back to Gilching, but Schendell said he was visiting friends in Starnberg and they would drive him back later. There was no mention of either the *Fragebogen* or the robbery.

I hurriedly left, before Schendell could, and drove quickly away. It wasn't until several months after the robbery, and only after Moser sent in innumerable reports asking for action, that Schendell finally was taken into custody. He was sentenced to a year's imprisonment. Ironically, his knowledge of and accessibility to automobiles stood him in good stead. A few years later he obtained a Ford franchise for the area and became a wealthy and influential man. Richard Freund told me, some time afterward on one of my visits to Germany, that several times over the years he and others had written to the Ford Motor Company expressing their opposition to Ford having given a franchise to a known Nazi who had probably been involved in atrocities and crimes against humankind as part of the SS, but that the Ford Motor Company never even gave them the courtesy of a reply. Richard wondered whether it was because Henry Ford had been a major Nazi supporter.

Richard Freund himself had several encounters with the U.S. Military Government that reinforced his perception that the MG appeared to favor Nazis at the expense of anti-Nazis and non-Nazis. One of the prominent Nazis residing in Gilching was a Dr. Andrews, who had held an important post in the government of the Third Reich. Freund had obtained copies of letters written by Andrews that described meetings he had had with Hitler and other high-ranking officials. In an attempt to bring Andrews to justice, shortly after the war was over Freund took the letters to the American MG in Starnberg and gave them to the secretary of the MG's head of security police, a Captain Shellenberger. Because there were no duplicating machines then, Freund wanted a receipt for the letters. The secretary asked one of Shellenberger's assistants, a Lieutenant Peden, to provide one, but Peden refused. He told Freund that if and when he wanted the letters back, he need only ask for them. About a month later, with Andrews still living freely in Gilching, Freund went to the Starnberg MG to find out the status of his complaint. He was told that no action had been taken. When Freund asked about the incriminating letters, he was told that no one had any information about them. When he asked for their return, he was told that they couldn't be found.

A further incident with the Starnberg MG convinced Freund that at least some of the American officers were Nazi sympathizers. Freund had owned an automobile before the war, which had been confiscated and given to a Dr. Paul, the German commandant of a nearby slave labor factory. When the first group of American soldiers arrived in Gilching, Freund went to the commanding officer, told him the story and showed him his original ownership papers, whereupon the automobile was taken from Paul and returned to him. MG law, in fact, would have dictated the confiscation of all of Paul's possessions, but Freund was satisfied to have his car back. For the next two months Freund used the car to provide dental care for anti-Nazis and non-Nazis in the area, who were denied service by almost all the other German doctors and dentists. Then a new military commander was assigned to the area, and as soon as the old one left, the mayor of Gilching, Johann Simon, ordered Freund to return the auto to Dr. Paul. Forced to comply, Freund went to the Starnberg MG, explained the circumstances and asked that the MG order Simon to have the car once again returned to him. The MG flatly refused to take any action, not even investigating to determine whether Freund's claim was valid.

But Freund wasn't to be deterred. He obtained a job as a dentist at the Oberpfaffenhofen air base. He wasn't permitted to do dental work for the Americans, but was assigned to do the work required by the German prisoners-of-war who were held at the base for some months following V-E Day. Freund obtained a letter from the medical officer he reported to, attesting to his need for a car to properly perform his dental duties, and he went once again to the Starnberg MG. At the MG office he was referred to a German civilian named Weisseger, who the MG had put in charge of all civilian automobile matters for the Starnberg district. Weisseger did not immediately turn down Freund's request, but prior to making a decision asked him a series of questions about himself and the history of the car's ownership. As soon as he learned that Freund was half-Jewish, Weisseger cursed the Jews and summarily ordered Freund out of his office. Despite complaints, the MG officer in charge took no action against Weisseger. Richard never did get his car back.

Many of the U.S. military bases, as well as USMG units, were reputed to be riddled with Nazism. At the air base in Kaufbeuren, I saw little overt pro-Nazi activity or support. An order did require that only German civilians must be hired and that displaced persons may not be hired. However, a number of D.P.s were working on the base because they were not living in designated displaced persons camps and had papers showing them to be residents of Germany.

The air base at Oberpfaffenhofen was different. Civilians working there and living in the vicinity called it the "Nazi Airfield." It was common knowledge that Germans who had been fired from jobs with other U.S. military or MG units because of pro-Nazi activity or previous records as Nazis were with few exceptions able to get jobs at this base.

I learned about it first from a Jewish survivor I met in Gilching. He told me that when he applied for a job at the Oberpfaffenhofen air base, he was required first to fill out a questionnaire about his background, including past political activities. He was refused a job and was given no reason. What disturbed him almost as much, he told me, was that while he was filling out the questionnaire he saw at least a half-dozen German civilians enter the personnel office, ask for jobs and receive them without so much as a single question of political affiliation being asked of them. Young, pretty women had no trouble at all getting jobs at the base. Beatrice Lindner had been fired from three different offices on the base because her supervisor objected to her out-spoken pro-Hitler and pro-Nazi proselytizing. Each time, how-ever, she managed to find a lonely officer in charge of a different office and was almost immediately rehired.

It was the practice at most American military installations in Germany to find a civilian who would supervise the other civilian employees. At Oberpfaffenhofen the man hired for this job was known in the area for his intense Nazi sympathies. His name was Rademacher and he arranged to have hired as one of his assistants a man named Tanofsky. Tanofsky had been a test pilot at this same base during the Nazi era and had belonged to the branch of the Nazi party called Sicherheit Dienst, the SD—the security forces—which some said were even more brutal than the Schutz Staffel, the SS—the elite Black Shirts.

Principally responsible for what appeared to be favoritism to-ward Nazi employees and discrimination against anti-Nazis and dis-placed persons was the officer in charge of personnel, Major Rich-ard Scott. Scott's chief interpreter was known as an avid Nazi, and although Scott was told repeatedly of the man's affiliations, he re-fused to acknowledge the charges or investigate the interpreter's background. Another officer stationed there, Lieutenant Albert L. Cusick, had repeatedly fought the growth of Nazism on the base

and, as best as he could considering his rank, the officers sympa-
thizing with it. Cusick found a photo of Scott's interpreter leading
a Nazi parade during the Hitler era. This photo, coupled with other
allegations regarding Scott's hiring of Nazis, prompted a demand
for an investigation of Major Scott and his operation of the personnel office. Before any probe could be undertaken, however, Scott
was quietly transferred. His replacement was a Captain Coit. Coit's
interpreter, a man named Krug, was also alleged to have Nazi sympathies. As chief interpreter for the new personnel officer, Krug
frequently was accused of giving false translations to Coit during
employment interviews. Many non-Nazis were denied work and
many Nazis were given jobs.

The military government and the Minister President of Germany, approved by the U.S. occupation authorities, had stated
that not only were bona-fide Nazi party members to be considered as Nazis, but those who may not have joined the party, yet
had openly supported the Nazi regime, were also to be considered Nazis. The U.S. occupation headquarters issued orders that
all Nazis who had held administrative positions in the Third Reich
and who were now working for the Americans were to be reduced
to the position of common laborer, and that any of these Nazis
who were known to have participated directly in any German
atrocities were to be summarily fired. On a number of bases, including Oberpfaffenhofen, this order was principally enforced not
by demoting or firing those in the higher civilian positions, but
by dismissing those in the lowest jobs. The commandant of the
Oberpfaffenhofen air base, Colonel Albert G. Hewitt, was asked
to explain why more thorough measures were not being taken to

rid the base of its Nazi elements. He replied that if those in the more important jobs were fired, as prescribed in the order, the civilian strength of the air base would be reduced by eighty percent or more.

U.S. Counter Intelligence Corps (CIC) units were established in a number of areas in occupied Germany to combat continuing Nazism in those areas. There was a CIC unit at Oberpfaffenhofen. It was informed by an anti-Nazi civilian group in Gilching that the former head of the airfield, who had sent to the concentration camps many of the slave laborers who had been forced to work at Oberpfaffenhofen, was living in complete freedom only ten miles from the base. The CIC was also given complete Nazi party membership lists of the area, with a request that the former party members be investigated and, where warranted, brought to justice. When I left Germany to return to the States, months after the CIC was given this information, no action had yet been taken. Another clear message from the U.S. to the Germans about Nazism was embodied in one of the first acts of Lieutenant General Lucius D. Clay when he became chief of the military government in the U.S. occupied zone, taking over the governing of Germany from the State Department some six months after the end of the war. Clay granted complete political amnesty to the approximately one million Nazis in Bavaria under 27 years of age—the Hitler *Jugend* who had been the educational and military backbone of the Third Reich.

When observing the efforts of the American occupation forces encountering the continuing Nazism in postwar Germany, one can't help but be reminded of one of Walt Kelly's *Pogo* comments: "We have met the enemy and they are us."

While there is no suggestion here that all or even most MG offices were operated like that at Starnberg or that many military bases were run like that at Oberpfaffenhofen, it was frightening for the victims of Nazism to believe—and satisfying for the Nazis to observe—that the U.S. forces that fought for almost four years against Nazism were now, often, apparently supporting the principles of an enemy it had sacrificed a quarter-million lives to defeat. For the Germans who might have been ready to turn from Nazism to a new order of American-style democracy, the actions of too many USMG offices suggested that it might be okay for them to hold onto their Nazi beliefs. These included continuing hatred, enmity and persecution of the Jewish survivors of the concentration camps. Many people, survivors and Germans both, were prompted to ask, "Who won this war, anyway?"

# Chapter 12 ～

## SALVATION

I had been in Oberpfaffenhofen only a week when I got the call from Ed Herman.

That morning the mail trucks started coming in from the Munich Bahnhof and by evening the chapel at the Kaufbeuren air base was full of packages. Hundreds of packages from all over the United States. It was as if a floodgate had been opened. Ed, with Chaplain Bond and Captain Jacobson, took charge of sorting and examining the packages. They would have the first batch delivered to St. Ottilien in a few days. I made sure I was there.

I couldn't wait to see the reaction of the survivors. I wanted to experience the pride and satisfaction firsthand. I helped open the cartons in a partially cleared area on the first floor of one the buildings. Clothes and food and medicine and prayer shawls and tefillim and yarmulkes. I tried to act as nonchalant as I could, but couldn't contain my excitement. I was overcome, as if I had been holding my breath for a long time and finally could begin to gulp down huge swallows of air. I tried to cover my tears with a broad grin. I probably looked silly. Ed and I stood there, watching, as one by one, two by two, ten by ten, staff and patients of

St. Ottilien came in to surround the growing pile of articles. They approached cautiously, carefully, as though it must be some kind of a trick, so they would not suffer the disappointment of an expectation that they were afraid to believe had truly come about. In a few minutes it seemed like the entire hospital had formed a semicircle around the pile of packages. No one spoke. Even the footsteps were hushed. Necks craned, shoulders hunched forward, eyes stared.

A few moved very slowly, a step at a time, from the edge of the crowd toward the packages, to take a closer look. They nodded in affirmation that what they saw was real, hesitated for a moment as though they were going to reach out and touch, and then, with their hands open and their elbows forcefully pulled back at their hips, they inched slowly backward into the crowd. For a long time, it seemed, although it may have been no more than a minute, there was absolute stillness of movement and sound, everyone waiting expectantly but no one seeming to know exactly for what. Then one man moved forward toward the packages, stood right in the center, then threw himself onto a pile of clothes, grabbed some in his hands, held them out as an offering to the crowd and shouted, dragging out each word as if he were proclaiming a great event, "What . . . are . . . we . . . waiting . . . for?" and threw the clothes into the air with a shout of triumph, clapping his hands above his head. With that, with one long cry of happiness in unison, "ay . . . yai . . . yai . . ." the people rushed toward the treasure, sat on the ground, on each other, bent over the boxes, holding, lifting, showing, twirling, exchanging, fondling, like children jumping into a bale of hay and finding it turned into multicolored ribbons of confetti.

Laughing, crying, dancing, hugging and kissing each other, it was as if they were showering in the first rain after years of drought. Yet each one handled every item with care and restraint. It was, they knew, their salvation, and nothing was to be damaged. They read the labels on the tins and boxes of food, tried on the sweaters and coats and hats, gingerly placed the medical supplies off to the side where they could not inadvertently be harmed, threw prayer shawls over their shoulders, twisted tefillim around their arms and placed yarmulkes on their heads. Medicine, bandages and medical instruments had been sent by individual doctors from all over the States. There were enough clothes and shoes and overcoats for most people at St. Ottilien to have a complete outfit for the winter. There seemed to be enough yarmulkes and prayer shawls and Bibles for all the fourteen thousand Jews left in the American zone in Bavaria. One synagogue in Cincinnati sent its own Torah. No one went off with anything, no one tried to put anything in a pocket, no one attempted to keep anything for their own. They enjoyed this manna from heaven together and would use it together, these life-saving, life-sharing things.

That evening I wrote home about this remarkable happening. Shortly after the liberation concert on May 27, I had begun writing home regularly about St. Otillien. As it turned out, it was a good thing I had done so.

By the time we found out why the packages had been so long in coming and why they suddenly arrived in such large numbers, Ed had also been transferred to Oberpfaffenhofen. We were delighted to be together again, and although we knew that our principal purpose had been accomplished, that the people of St. Ottilien would survive the fast-approaching winter, we also knew that our commitment was not over; now we had to make sure not only that material aid continued but that the survivors would be helped in their next step up the ladder to a sane civilization: locating any loved ones who remained alive, joining family members in the United States and other countries, and—for most of them, who were totally alone in the world—emigration to Palestine.

By the 21st of October over fifteen hundred packages had arrived for St. Ottilien, more than enough to meet its needs. Many of the packages had been sent by organizations and were the maximum seventy-pound weight limit. With Ed no longer at Kaufbeuren, Chaplain Bond and Captain Jacobson continued to sort and deliver packages. There were so many and so much, they were able to distribute some food, clothes and medicine to a number of other camps in the U.S. zone of Germany. Ironically, the Jewish Welfare Board, one of the organizations to whom Dr. Grinberg had written and from whom he reported receiving no aid, shipped some of the larger packages after Leonard Herman sent them the letter and phoned them.

By the end of the month Ed and I learned that not only had our letter resulted in the shipment of the supplies, but it had played a key role in the reversal of United States policy towards the Jewish survivors still in Germany and Austria.

The information came to us principally in letters from my

mother and from Ed's brother, Leonard. Accompanying the letters was an article from the front page of *The New York Times* of September 30, 1945. From the letters, the *Times* article and copies of correspondence, mainly between Leonard and several organizations, we pieced together much of the story.

It appeared that at some point our letter had reached the White House. Leonard had made special efforts to get the letter circulated to prominent people both in and out of government. He got it to influential Jews, especially those with strong political connections. We later heard, but never could verify, that it might have been New York Senator Herbert Lehman who brought the letter to the attention of President Truman. We also heard that Truman was disturbed by the letter. He had publicly expressed sympathy for the concentration camp victims, survivors and other displaced persons, and, we were told, he found it difficult to believe the allegations that they were being starved and mistreated inside the American occupation zone by the Americans.

We were later told that Truman asked Dean Earl Harrison to investigate the charges in our letter and to check out our backgrounds and motives. In the meantime, we were also later informed, the President ordered the shipments for St. Ottilien to be held up at the port of embarkation, pending verification of our allegations.

The clipping from *The New York Times*\* explained what had happened. The headline read: "PRESIDENT ORDERS EISENHOWER TO END NEW ABUSE OF JEWS." The sub-

---

\* See appendix

head continued: "Acting on Harrison Report, He Likens Our Treatment to That of the Nazis." And below that: "Conditions for Displaced in Reich Called Shocking."

The story, datelined September 29, Washington, D.C., stated that President Truman had acted on the basis of the report made by Dean Harrison, which detailed the conditions we had described in our letter: how the survivors were being held behind barbed wire in camps guarded by American Military Police, how conditions were unsanitary and the food poor and insufficient, how the displaced persons were without adequate medical care or medicine, and how many of them were still forced to wear their concentration camp uniforms because they had no other clothing. "All were wondering," the story stated, "if they had been liberated after all, and were despairing of help."

When Ed and I read the *Times* story we embraced and, indulging our own egos for a moment, shouted, "We did it!"

A letter from my mother told more of the story. "Dean Earl Harrison came to visit me last month," my mother wrote. "He wanted to know about you. President Truman, he told me, was concerned about the letters you and Ed Herman have been sending all over the country. Dean Harrison said it was impossible to believe that all the things you wrote could be true, and he wanted to find out what kind of person you were. You know what I did? You know all those letters you've been writing home these past months about St. Ottilien? I keep them in the top drawer of one of the little dressers in my bedroom. I gave him the letters. He sat down on the living room couch and began reading. After about twenty minutes he gave them back to me and said, 'I believe it.'

What you wrote in the letter was what you wrote in the letters you sent me. He seemed relieved that you and Ed Herman were telling the truth. He said he would make a personal inspection of the conditions and report back to President Truman."

Though even in later years my mother continued to insist that her visitor had been Dean Harrison himself, I was never quite sure that he would have personally taken the time to check out a 20-year-old army private. I've always thought that it must have been an assistant sent by Harrison, and that the excitement of the moment had left my mother confused. On the other hand, maybe my mother was right.

One of the documents we received from Leonard Herman was a copy of a letter addressed to him from Murray Le Vine, Executive Director of HIAS (Hebrew Immigrant Aid Society) of Philadelphia. The letter, dated October 1, 1945, stated in part that Ed's and my letter "was placed in the hands of Mr. Earl G. Harrison, who as you know, is a United States member under the Interdepartmental Review Committee . . . and something is being done . . . I did not want to do anything until Mr. Harrison's report to the President broke the press, as you probably noticed . . . the *Times* and most every paper in the country . . . published the situation."

Leonard also enclosed a story from *Time* magazine of October 8, 1945, that included the following:

"General Eisenhower [said in a report this week that] '. . . it is not easy for the local MG officer to dismiss the only waterworks engineer in his city because he was an active Nazi. The decision must be made, however. . . .'

"The hard fact," the *Time* article continued, "was that many U.S. officers in Germany refused to make the decision. Many believed, with [General] George Patton, that there was no point in trying to make it.

"Plain GIs had their problems too. Ever since they had come to Germany, the soldiers had fraternized—not only with Fraulein but with a philosophy. Many now began to say that the Germans were really OK, that they had been forced into the war, that the atrocity stories were fakes. Familiarity with the eager German women, the fresh-faced German young, bred forgetfulness of Belsen and Buchenwald and Oswiecizm.

"Tending more and more to accept the Germans, the Americans did not really impress the Germans. The plain truth was that Americans in Germany, as a group and as representatives of a great power, were serving neither themselves nor America well."

Following this background, the *Time* article discussed the Harrison report:

"[President Truman] released a dynamitic report from former U.S. Immigration Commissioner Earl G. Harrison, whom he had sent to investigate the fate of displaced persons, particularly Jews. Harrison's report pulled no punches. He charged that displaced Jews are being held in unsanitary, barbed-wire camps, wearing hideous concentration-camp garb or German SS uniforms, with nothing being done for them by way of rehabilitation. Their guards are U.S. troops.

"Harrison went further: 'Beyond knowing that they are no longer in danger of the gas chambers, torture and other forms of violent death, they see—and there is—little change . . . As matters now stand, we appear to be treating the Jews as the Nazis treated them, except that we do not exterminate them . . . One is led to wonder whether the German people, seeing this, are not supposing that we are following or at least condoning Nazi policy.'

". . . To General Dwight D. Eisenhower, the President sent a copy of this sizzling document, with an equally sizzling letter. Wrote the President: Policies for displaced persons are not being carried out by some subordinate officers; henceforth humane policies must be applied in the field; General Eisenhower must report back to the President as soon as possible on the steps he takes."

On the evening that we received the *Times* article, Ed and I gathered together some of the officers and men who had been working with St. Ottilien, to share with them not only the great news, but mutual relief and satisfaction. We read the story aloud in its entirety.

After most of the group had left, a few of us speculated on what the meeting between President Truman and Earl Harrison might have been like after Harrison confirmed the truth of the charges in our letter. We pictured President Truman sitting at his desk talking to Dean Harrison. A couple of us made up their dialogue as we went along. The visit of the colonel from SHAEF clearly had not endeared General Eisenhower to any of us.

"That sonuvabitch Eisenhower," we imagined Truman saying. "He used to be a poor kid and should have some sympathy for those starving D.P.s. But over there in Paris you forget who you are. Playing golf all day and drinking all night and doing who-the-hell-knows-what with that English woman he takes along as his driver everywhere he goes, he doesn't have time left to do what he's supposed to do. If he wasn't so damned popular, I'd fire the bastard. I'm going to phone him personally, and if he doesn't clean up this mess, I'm going to kick his ass."

"It's not all Ike's fault, Mr. President," Dean Harrison might have said. "His orders haven't been carried out."

"Is he the Supreme Commander or is he not the Supreme Commander? He's good at smoothing things over and getting people to work with him when he has to. Doesn't he have enough commitment to act except in a crisis?"

"You know how General Patton was, Mr. President. It was difficult for Ike to deal with him."

"I know that sonuvabitch Patton thought he was playing some kind of game. If he didn't have an enemy to fight, he didn't know where the hell he was or what was going on. So he invents an enemy. The commies and Jews. Remember what he told his troops? Kill the men and fuck the women. With the war over the Germans become his friends and he makes the D.P.s his enemies. Sure, I know it's tough to deal with Patton. But Ike ought to have the balls to do it."

"General Marshall has full confidence in Eisenhower, Mr. President."

"Marshall made him what he is. Yet I wouldn't be surprised that if some day the going got rough, Eisenhower would turn his back even on Marshall. Anyway, Earl, that's not solving our problem of what to do with the Jews and the other displaced persons. We need immediate action. This is getting to be a political hot potato and I'm holding it."

"You have my report, Mr. President. I will follow through with whatever you ask."

"First, I'm going to make your report public. And I don't give a damn if Eisenhower likes it or not. And then I want you to get over to Paris and tell Ike from me, personally, to put some balls on and get his generals to carry out his orders—and mine."

In later years we learned that our fantasy of a meeting between Truman and Harrison may not have been so fanciful, after all. In his book, *Truman*, David McCullough reported that both Eisenhower and Patton were bitter over Truman's ascendance to the presidency when Franklin Roosevelt died, and that Patton wrote: "It seems very unfortunate that in order to secure political preference, people are made Vice President who are never intended, neither by Party nor by the Lord to be Presidents."

Truman's support of the Jews and a Jewish homeland was well-known by the time he became President. In a 1943 speech he strongly attacked the "Nazi beasts'" intentions to slaughter not only the Jews of Europe, but other innocent peoples. "This is not a Jewish problem," he said, "it is an American problem."

His 1945 order to Eisenhower to change U.S. policy toward the survivors would not be the last time that Truman put Eisenhower in his place. Bert Cochran, in his book *Harry Truman and the Crisis Presidency*, indicates that Truman sometimes considered Eisenhower too close to "military nonsense," and that Truman understood in a more practical way how to deal with problems. Roy Jenkins, in his book *Truman*, notes that Truman never forgave Eisenhower for his treatment of General George Marshall during Ike's election campaign in 1952, when Eisenhower succumbed to the pressures of McCarthyism. Jenkins states that "Truman treated almost everything [Eisenhower] did . . . as being intolerable." This included a written accusation that Eisenhower's stand on restricting immigration endorsed "the practices of the 'master race,' and discriminated against Jews and Catholics."

So even if it didn't happen exactly the way we imagined it, we enjoyed the idea that two privates, Edward Herman and I, were at least in part responsible for a President publicly criticizing a general.

# Chapter 13 ～

## AFTERMATH

That Christmas season in Germany in 1945 was a good one for me. Few of the people I had known at St. Ottilien were still there. Most had either recovered and left, to salvage what they could of their lives, or were waiting for papers authorizing them to enter an immigration camp to join a family member they had discovered in some far-off country. Emigration was to wherever they were permitted to go, to whatever country was willing to allow them in, away from the ashes of Europe: Australia, China, England, Brazil, Canada, South Africa, the United States—although some of these had restrictive immigration policies, in large part aimed against Jews—and, most especially, if they could get there, Palestine.

I was certain that no one at St. Ottilien was going to starve that winter, and even as the cold weather began sweeping down from the north neither were they going to suffer from lack of clothing. I think it was Dee who managed to buy some geese from a nearby farm, and on Christmas Day we got a jeep and played Santa Claus to some of the D.P.s who worked on the base. Several of us piled into a jeep, geese piled up on the floor, and drove up and down the Bavarian hills, horn tooting, voices singing Christmas carols and jeep wheels screeching around ice-hard corners. I played

"Silent Night" on one of the harmonicas Ed had given me from a shipment he had bought in the Black Forest in Germany and sold in Paris. One of our stops was at the Remmler house, where we dropped off a goose for the Freunds to cook and share with Miriam, Adele and Katie. I saw the girls frequently and continued to encourage them about their upcoming migration to the States. They still had not been notified to report to one of the immigration centers.

Food was still the most precious commodity in Germany, but its availability to the Germans had increased significantly in the past two months. Although the war had been over for more than half a year, the German economy had not yet begun to function independently of the American occupation forces and it was, ironically, precisely because of this that more food was available. The continuing return home of American soldiers decreased the food requirements of the armed forces. Because adjustments in supply shipments always lagged behind the changing needs, there was a small but steady surplus constantly arriving at most bases. Although large quantities of food and other materials destined for troops stationed in Germany and elsewhere continued to be siphoned off in increasingly efficient and flourishing black market operations in Paris and other quartermaster depot cities, the same proportionate amount got through to their destinations for use on local black markets. Substantial amounts nevertheless reached the officially designated recipients.

In addition, President Truman's order to General Eisenhower to provide adequate care for displaced persons resulted in less need for the D.P.s and sympathetic American soldiers to beg, liberate or scrounge food by intimidation from German civilian sources. Although the Bürgermeisters of most of the small cities and towns continued to manipulate food resources to favor those Germans they had known as loyal and active Nazis, they now had more supplies for the general population. The Germans had potatoes, flour, some meat from the restocked cattle herds, and with the reactivation of breweries and distilleries by the U.S. Army to serve its own needs, plenty of beer and schnapps.

It was not, of course, the *gemütlichkeit* of the Hitler years. In the cities many people still lived on the open floors of bombed, skeletal buildings with makeshift walls and ceilings. In the country many people lived in barns and in hastily constructed shacks. But there seemed to be few in danger of starvation at this Christmas time of 1945.

Most of the displaced persons in the U.S. zone, following the Harrison report and the Truman orders, were receiving at least 1,200 calories per day and had sufficient clothing and medicine to keep them alive through the winter. In addition, the barbed wire was removed from all D.P. camps.

But all was not entirely well. The Jews and *auslander* were facing a new threat. The reluctance of the American military government to disavow and punish known Nazis on the local level, and the retention of Nazi officials in their bureaucratic jobs, from Bürgermeister on down, gave new hope to the Hitler supporters following the first few months of despair after the end of the war. Contingents of Military Police remained at many D.P. camps. However, they were no longer there to imprison the D.P.s, but to protect them from the anti-Semitic and anti-foreigner violence of these revived Nazi civilian groups, particularly the bands of young men in their early and middle 20s who terrorized anti-Nazis throughout Germany, the "werewolves." The survivors, including those at St. Ottilien, knew it was time to leave Germany once and for all, and they renewed their efforts to find a way to emigrate.

I left Germany in February 1946, for discharge in the States. Before I left, I arranged with a fellow GI, Bob Kingsbury, and with my roommate, Dee DiBiase, who would be staying some time longer, to follow up with Ed Herman on getting the sisters through the bureaucracy and to the U.S. They did, and the sisters arrived a few months later.

Ed Herman was discharged in May and chose to stay in Europe, where he had already developed a thriving import-export business between France and Germany and other countries, reviving trade that had been dormant since the beginning of the war except for Germany's use of its occupied countries' goods. Ed settled in Paris, working hard to make his first million, which he did in an even shorter time than he had predicted.

We had often talked about the fate of the survivors who had no relatives who could bring them to the United States or other countries where they might begin a new, peaceful life, and whose only alternative was to migrate to the soon-to-be state of Eretz-Israel. Ed and I both felt that the surviving Jews should be able to have some homeland where they could feel reasonably safe from another Holocaust. We evaluated the options in Europe at that time. In England, we agreed, Prime Minister Clement Atlee's attempts at limiting immigration from British dominion countries, with slogans like "India for the Indians," exacerbated an already growing anti-Jewish move-

ment. The irony was that Britain also did everything it could to prevent the Jewish survivors from reaching what they considered their
country. The collaboration of France and most French people with
the Nazis was a clear continuation of the Dreyfus syndrome that
existed in that country, making it difficult for Jews to live there. The
eastern European countries, such as Poland, which had had the largest Jewish populations, continued to applaud Hitler for ridding their
countries of those they simultaneously labeled international bank-
ers and revolutionary Bolsheviks.

Any survivor who went back to his or her Eastern European
home had a good chance of being murdered. Of the relative handful of survivors of Poland's three-and-half-million prewar Jewish
population, about a thousand were murdered in postwar attacks by
Polish civilians. An example was the July 4, 1946, massacre of forty-
two Jews in Kielce by a mob of civilians abetted by the military.
The Poles besieged a house that was sheltering Jewish groups, including thirty-five orphans preparing to leave for Palestine. Polish
soldiers forced the residents out of the building into the street where
the crowd beat them with iron bars and stones. The police stood
by and watched as women and children, as well as men, were slain.
Fifty years later, in 1996, Polish Prime Minister Wlodzimierz
Cimoszewicz publicly apologized for his country, stating that the
Kielce murders "came when the smoke of the crematoria still hung
over the land . . . when all that was left of Poland's Jewish minority was a handful of war-weary refugees and survivors."

It was not surprising, then, that living in Europe for several
years after the war, Ed Herman became involved in the smuggling
of Jews to Palestine.

Some of the survivors who were at St. Ottilien did make it to Palestine. By hiding in trucks and cars and even wagons they managed to get across the German border into France, past both the American Military Police and the French soldiers at border-crossing posts. Once in France they made their way to Marseilles. There they located a member of one of the three Jewish groups in Palestine fighting for a Jewish state and seeking to smuggle in Jews from all over the world—including survivors from Europe—past the British blockade. The three groups were the Hagganah, the principal army; the Irgun, the unofficial underground; and the Stern Gang, which functioned as a terrorist organization. Each needed more fighters.

The next step was to get on board one of the "ghost ships" that tried to make its way through the Mediterranean, evade the blockade and reach the shores of Eretz-Israel. Sometimes they were successful, sometimes they were turned back and sometimes they met with tragedy when the British used gunfire to stop them.

Many made it and found a new home.

Many did not.

In March 1946 I reentered civilian life. I liked to think then that I had contributed something important to making the lives of the concentration camp survivors better in U.S.-occupied Germany, and that perhaps I had even saved some from continued genocide by neglect. I wanted to begin my own adult life and to put the burden of worry and responsibility for the survivors behind me. I wanted to think that things were now better for them and with the springtime of 1946 offering new life and hope, that the years of continuing suffering, degradation and fear were finally over.

Things did get better at most displaced persons camps, including St. Ottilien, with the survivors slowly regaining some measure of control over their own lives. In some camps, despite Truman's orders to Eisenhower, insensitivity, prejudice and harassment continued. On March 27, 1946, shortly after I returned to the States, I read a newspaper story that General Lucien K. Truscott of the Third U.S. Army ordered the Ore Chadesch displaced persons camp at Fuerth, Germany, closed. At this camp some surviving Jews who had found members of their families alive were living in small houses. Although sparsely furnished, the houses afforded the survivors, for the first time in many years, something approximating family life. Truscott's order forced these families back into barracks, with as many as fifty people to a room. When I learned about this, I remembered Dr. Grinberg's liberation concert speech and his account of the initial protests of the Jews against Nazi laws, demanding their homes back and the right to continue to live as families. Now, with the war over for almost a year and the Nazi armies defeated, the Jewish survivors at Fuerth, eighteen hundred of them, marched and shouted once again, this time to the Americans: "Give us back the homes the Nazis stole from us . . . we demand the right to again enjoy family life." They pleaded: "We've been five years in concentration camps. We've suffered enough. Let us stay here quietly." The answer was the arrest and trial of those who refused to move.

Things seemed to have come full circle. Even under the Americans there seemed to be no exit.

Fifty years later things seem to have come full circle once again. The U.S. legacy not only permitted but encouraged the continuation of Nazism, albeit at various times underneath the surface, in postwar Germany. Although after World War II there was a public rush to atonement by Germany and a public rush to righteousness by the United States, in fact these countries' actions did not match their words. The strongest protests against neo-Nazism in Germany were taken by its young people who came to maturity in the 1960s. They added to their generation's worldwide struggle for peace, the environment and individual rights their own horror of the guilt of their parents' generation. They swore that they would never let it happen again.

Yet, in 1990s Germany, it appeared to be happening again. In part the Cold War reinforced the concept of violence against those whose political philosophies disagreed with ours. The Cold War also reinforced the Nazi claim that the real world enemy was communism, and the United States' strengthening of that argument gave additional justification for the growth of neo-Nazi groups. Germany has not reached the age of the "skinheads" in a vacuum.

U.S. Congressman Joseph Kennedy put it in perspective when he said during a December 1992, visit to Germany that "the problem cannot be swept under the rug. The issue is not four thousand neo-Nazis [but] the hidden, silent support of people and lack of drive by the German government and citizens to put an end to it." He added that "there is a whole segment of the [German] cabinet that is operating under a mentality of denial."

In April 1994, Douglas H. Jones, senior officer in the United States Embassy's Berlin office, stated: "If I were a skinhead, I would take a certain amount of comfort in hearing [from Chancellor Helmut Kohl] that Germany is not a country of immigration." He condemned German xenophobia in terms reminiscent of criticisms by those few diplomats in the 1930s courageous enough to point out the true state of the Emperor's clothes.

The leaders of much of the rest of the world, including the United States, appear willing to repeat history. By mirroring the silence of the 1930s and countenancing by polite denunciation the neo-Nazism of the present time, they are setting the stage for a repetition of the hate that marked World War II and its attendant genocide.

The lack of action by so-called democratic and humanitarian countries to stop genocide in other parts of the world not only exacerbates but lends credence to the belief that in our race for material gain we prefer neither to remember the past nor to learn from it. That way we can disclaim responsibility for tragedies that we might be able to stop, just as the world did nothing about the plight of the Jews during the Holocaust and ignored their continuing struggle to survive under the Americans after their liberation. How many years did we permit genocide to run rampant in Bosnia before we took action to stop it? How many years did it take before the American public finally put a stop to the bombing and burning of tens of thousands of innocent victims, including children, in Vietnam? What did we do to intervene in Idi Amin's slaughter of hundreds of thousands in Uganda? What actions did we take to stop the mass murder of hundreds of thousands, perhaps millions, in Rwanda, in Burundi, in Liberia? How much effort are we willing to make to stop the abolition or infringement of people's civil rights whenever we learn about it, wherever it may be and whoever they may be, whether Jews, Palestinians, Chinese, Kurds, Mayans,

Nigerians or, in many countries of the world, women? About as much, perhaps, as was done for the Jews in Germany during the Hitler years?

The United States is not immune. Our history of genocide against Native Americans, brutality against African-Americans and discrimination against other racial, ethnic and religious groups has spawned, in the 1990s, our own "skinhead" movement of organized neo-Nazis and armed militias that threaten not only specific targets but all of us.

The world forgets. Those of us who remember or who are concerned about what we have learned of the Holocaust must do everything we can to make certain that the rest of the world does not forget, and that genocide—whether deliberate or by neglect—should never happen again, to anyone, anytime, anywhere.

# Appendix ◄—

## REPORT BY THE JEWISH CENTRAL INFORMATION OFFICE

JEWISH CENTRAL INFORMATION OFFICE
19, Manchester Square
LONDON, W. 1

25 August, 1945

### The Jews of Berlin

The following data are based on a talk with the
chairman of the Berlin Jewish Community, Mr. Erich
Nehlhans

1. Number of Jews on August 15, 1945

    a)   "Full Jews" ("Volljuden") .................................................. 3,000

         "Bearers of the Badge" ("Sterntrager") .......................... 2,000
         This group includes Jews married to non-Jews and
         "mixed breeds" ("Mischlinge") of the Jewish faith.
        Of these 5,000, 960 returned from concentration camps,
        underground, i.e. without papers, with forged papers or
        officially believed to be "Aryans."

    b)   In addition to Jews as under a), there are some 2 to 3,000 "Full
        Jews" not of the Jewish faith, but declared to be Jews by the
        Nazis in or after 1933. They are not members of the newly
        constituted Jewish community and do not consider themselves
        to be Jews.

    c)   "Mixed breeds" ("Mischlinge") not of the Jewish faith: their
        number is unknown.

2. Nationality

Most Jews under 1a, and all under 1b, are of German birth and nationality. Some were stateless before 1933, some are of Polish birth.

3. Organization of the Jewish Community

a) There is one organized body. It is responsible for
   1. synagogues and religious services
   2. financing the relief of the destitute
   3. religious instruction and professional retraining (which has hardly begun)
   4. The administration of hospitals, homes, and a transit camp.

b) The Jewish community still owns considerable funds. These amounted to RM 3,500,000 in April, 1945. They were blocked, like all German-owned bank deposits, by order of the Allied authorities in May and have not been released since.

c) Needs of the Jewish Community:
   1. Release of blocked bank accounts to support Jews out of work and 6 to 7,000 refugees mainly from the territory east of the Oder. The rates are RM/35 for single persons; RM/65 for married couples. This is being financed at the moment through private borrowing. This is being financed at the moment through private borrowing.
   2. Food, clothing, bedding, is needed by all members of the community, especially by those returned from concentration camps.
   3. Liaison with the military authorities, i.e. Military Government: there is none yet. There is no welfare department of Military Government. No Military Government officer ever contacted the Jewish community. An American rabbi and Dr. Levy, of the British Army, called on the chairman a fortnight ago and promised help.

4. Synagogues, Hospitals, Homes

All synagogues having been destroyed, there are only temporary synagogues. Of those there are five. Services are held. There is a large Jewish hospital in Iranische Strasse, which was permitted even under the Nazis. It is in fairly good condition but like all Berlin hospitals is short of medical supplies and food. A transit-camp has been set up. Eligible for admission are invalids, homeless persons and Jews from concentration camps awaiting repartition to other parts of Germany.

5. Experiences of Individual Jews

Though these are too well known to require elaboration, a few points are perhaps worth mentioning. "Full Jews" and "Sternträger" who escaped arrest owe their survival in Berlin to official oversight, essential work at the hospital or going underground. Others succeeded in bribing the Gestapo officials sent to deport them. Mr. Nehlhans managed to rescue himself and 36 others by paying RM 5,000 per head, with the proviso that they should all disappear. Those living underground had no ration cards and had to rely on the charity of "Aryans." Mr. Nehlhans was harbored for two years by an "Aryan" family in Magdeburg.

6. What Do Those Jews Think?

They are deeply disappointed that liberation has not fulfilled the hopes which it has raised. What mortifies them most is the indifference shown by the British and American authorities. Secretly listening for years to the B.B.C., to its indictment of Nazi atrocities, expressions of sympathy and promises of help, they were led to believe that the end of Nazism would be followed by immediate relief and rehabilitation. The survivors feel that little has changed since the Russians entered Berlin, except that food supply is even shorter. They are still a stricken minority, unrelieved and uncared for by anybody, which is rapidly nearing the limits of human endurance. Mr. Nehlhans feels that unless help arrives quickly, the problem of the Jews of Berlin will be largely solved by suicide and death.

7. Needs of the Jews

    a)   FOOD. Unless imprisoned for political reasons, Jews do not qualify for rations as per top scale. Considering the inadequacy of food during the last six years owing to discrimination or inability to obtain ration cards, Jews feel that some allowances should be made now.

    b)   CLOTHING and BLANKETS. Jews do not even have the bare minimum owing to confiscation (of both material and clothing coupons) and deportation. Clothing and blankets are unobtainable in Germany now.

c) JOBS. Some employers are still afraid of the Nazis and reluctant to employ Jews. Jews are not appointed to positions of responsibility in local government. The head of the "Sozialamt" for the whole of Berlin, Dr. Geschke, a member of the Communist Party with a record of twelve years in a concentration camp, stated that membership in the Jewish race or faith does not constitute a claim to a good position in local administration. Members of the Communist and Social Democratic Parties come first, and there is evidently no sense of fellowship between them as victims of Fascism on the one side and Jews as such on the other.

d) A representation of Jewish interests through a special department of German local government does not exist.

e) Contacting next-of-kin abroad: there are no facilities whatever, except with the help of soldiers forwarding letters.

8. Jews in Other Parts of Eastern Germany

BRESLAU: 2,000 are reported to have survived or returned. The Russians do not help them. An appeal to their Jewish brethren in Berlin had to be rejected because the community there was unable to help.

In the annexed territories membership in the Jewish community is not usually a protection from expulsion or expropriation.

"All the News That's Fit to Print"

# The New York Times

NEWS INDEX, PAGE 47, THIS SECTION

VOL. XCV..No. 32,026.    Entered as Second-Class Matter, Postoffice, New York, N. Y.    NEW YORK, SUNDAY, SEPTEMBER 30, 1945.    Copyright, 1945, by The New York Times Company.

# PRESIDENT ORDERS EISENHOWER TO END NEW ABUSE OF JEWS

## He Acts on Harrison Report, Which Likens Our Treatment to That of the Nazis

## MAKES PLEA TO ATTLEE

## Urges Opening of Palestine— Conditions for Displaced in Reich Called Shocking

*The text of the report on displaced persons, Page 38.*

**By BERTRAM D. HULEN**
Special to The New York Times.

WASHINGTON, Sept. 29—President Truman has directed General Eisenhower to clean up alleged shocking conditions in the treatment of displaced Jews in Germany, outside the Russian zone and in Austria. He acted on the basis of a report made by Earl G. Harrison, American representative on the Intergovernmental Committee on Refugees, after an inspection.

The report declared that displaced Jews were held behind barbed wire in camps guarded by our men, camps in which frequently conditions were unsanitary and the food poor and insufficient, with our military more concerned with other matters.

Some of the displaced Jews were sick and without adequate medicine, the report stated, and many had to wear prison garb or, to their chagrin, German SS uniforms. All were wondering, it was added, if they had been liberated after all and were despairing of help while worrying about the fate of relatives.

### Formal Appeal to Attlee

The President appealed formally to Prime Minister Attlee of Great Britain to open the doors of Palestine to 100,000 displaced Jews of Germany and Austria who want to be evacuated there.

Mr. Harrison, dean of the University of Pennsylvania Law School and former Immigration Commissioner, submitted his report at a personal conference with President Truman in August. The President wrote to General Eisenhower Aug. 31. In the communication he cited the following paragraph from Mr. Harrison's report:

"As matters now stand, we appear to be treating the Jews as the Nazis treated them except that we do not exterminate them. They are in concentration camps in large numbers under our own military guard instead of SS troops. One is led to wonder whether the German people, seeing this, are not supposing that we are following or at least condoning Nazi policy."

The report, while praising "some" of our Army officers in Germany for their handling of the Jews, for the most part severely arraigned the way they were dealing with the problem.

President Truman declared in his letter to General Eisenhower that policies promulgated by Supreme Headquarters, Allied Expeditionary Forces, "are not being carried out by some of your subordinate officers."

*The New York Times* September 30, 1945 front page story of the Harrison report and Truman's orders to Eisenhower. REPRINTED BY PERMISSION OF *THE NEW YORK TIMES*

**Policy Declared Violated**

The announced policy of giving the "liberated" prisoners preference in billeting among the German civilian population had not been followed on "a wide scale," he asserted.

"We must intensify our efforts," he wrote, "to get these people out of camps and into decent houses until they can be repatriated or evacuated."

He also asked General Eisenhower to carry out a suggestion of Mr. Harrison for more extensive field visitations by the Army and adequate inspections so that conditions could be promptly and effectively corrected.

"We must make clear to the German people that we thoroughly abhor the Nazi policies of hatred and persecution," he stated. "We have no better opportunity to demonstrate this than by the manner in which we ourselves actually treat the survivors remaining in Germany."

General Eisenhower had replied, the White House said, that he was investigating the conditions and would report to the President.

The President had not yet heard from Mr. Attlee on the Palestine question, the White House added, and the President's letter to Mr. Attlee was not given out pending a reply.

Mr. Harrison reported that the conditions affecting the displaced Jews as he observed them were such that unless remedies were applied there was danger of trouble.

They were held in many cases, he said, behind barbed wire camps formerly used by the Germans for their prisoners, including the notorious Berger Belsen camp. Nearly all had lost hope, he stated.

The Germans in rural areas, whom the Jews look out upon from the camps, were better fed, better clothed and better housed than the "liberated" Jews, the report declared.

Unless proper remedial action was taken and promptly, Mr. Harrison warned, "substantial unofficial and unauthorized movements of people must be expected and these will require considerable force to prevent." It could not be overemphasized, he cautioned, that "many of these people are now desperate."

Mr. Harrison urged the opening of Palestine to the displaced Jews, most of whom are Polish, Baltic, Hungarian or Rumanian, in addition to German and Austrian. He declared that the issue of Palestine "must be faced" and voiced hope that we could persuade Britain to make a "reasonable extension or modification" of her White Paper of 1939 which permitted Jewish immigration into Palestine on a limited basis.

There was no acceptable or even decent solution for the future of many European Jews other than Palestine, he contended, adding that his position was "purely humanitarian" and taken with "no reference to ideological or political considerations."

He also urged that the United States admit a "reasonable" number of these Jews under our existing immigration law. Some wanted to come here and others to go to England, the Dominions and South Africa, he added, explaining that the number desiring to enter the United States was not large.

Mr. Harrison urged that "those who have suffered most and longest" receive "first and not last attention" now, that the mass repatriation had been so largely completed. Evacuation from Germany, he said, should be "the emphasized theme" and the Jews so wishing should be permitted to return to their own countries without further delay.

Referring to the expiration of immigration certificates for Palestine in August, he stated:

"It is nothing short of calamitous to contemplate that the gates of Palestine should soon be closed."

He quoted Hugh Dalton to show that the British Labor party had stood for a liberal policy on this question.

Those displaced Jews not able to leave the country, Mr. Harrison declared, should be gotten out of the camps and the ill placed in tuberculosis sanitaria or in rest homes. Others should be billeted with the Germans while those who wished to be in camps should be placed in separate ones.

"There seems little justification," he asserted, "for the continuance of barbed-wire fences, armed guards and prohibition against leaving the camp except by passes."

He recommended that as quickly as possible the operations of such camps as remain be turned over to the UNRRA.

Since military authorities must necessarily continue to participate in the program, he urged that there be a review of military personnel selected for camp commandant positions with the aim of obtaining sympathetic officers. Pending the creation of this setup, he suggested that there be more extensive field visitations.

The Combined Displaced Persons Executive, Mr. Harrison said, had generally followed nationality lines, feeling that to treat the Jews separately would make for intolerance and trouble on the part of others. He called this an "unrealistic approach."

Their former barbaric persecution, he pointed out, had made the Jews a separate group with greater needs.

Because of preoccupation with the mass repatriations and with various difficulties, Mr. Harrison reported, the military authorities had shown considerable resistance to the entrance of voluntary agencies on the scene. In a few places "fearless and uncompromising" military officers had requisitioned whole villages for Jews or required them to be billeted by the Germans, but "at many places" our officers had manifested "the utmost reluctance or indisposition, if not timidity, about inconveniencing the German population."

These officers contend, the report stated, that their job is to get the communities going again while the displaced persons constitute a temporary problem. This has re-

sulted, it was added, in a burgomeister easily persuading a town major to give shabby places with improper facilities to Jews while saving better accommodations for returning German civilians.

"This tendency," Mr. Harrison reported, "reflects itself in other ways, namely, in the employment of German civilians in the offices of Military Government officers when equally qualified personnel could easily be found among the displaced persons whose repatriation is not imminent.

"Actually there have been situations where displaced persons, especially Jews, have found it difficult to obtain audiences with Military Government authorities because, ironically, they have been obliged to go through German employes who have not facilitated matters."

There had been some general improvement in conditions, Mr. Harrison reported, but there had been relatively little done beyond the planning stage.

Many of the Jews, the report said, had no opportunity, except surreptitiously, to communicate with the outside world.

The diet was principally bread and coffee, the report stated, and there are many pathetic malnutrition cases.

Mr. Harrison estimated there would be more than 1,000,000 displaced persons in Germany and Austria this winter, in many instances housed in buildings unfit for cold weather.

"All the News
That's Fit to Print"

# The New York Times

NEWS INDEX, PAGE 47, THIS SECTION
VOL. XCV..No. 32,026.    Entered as Second-Class Matter, Postoffice, New York, N. Y.    Copyright, 1945, by The New York Times Company.
NEW YORK, SUNDAY, SEPTEMBER 30, 1945.

# REPORT IS SENT TO EISENHOWER

### President Stresses Responsibility to Refugees and Policies of Potsdam and SHAEF

*Special to The New York Times.*

WASHINGTON, Sept. 29—The text of President Truman's letter to General Eisenhower on the report of Earl G. Harrison on displaced persons in Germany and Austria was as follows:

Aug. 31, 1945.

"My Dear General Eisenhower:

"I have received and considered the report of Mr. Earl G. Harrison, our representative on the Intergovernmental Committee on Refugees, upon his mission to inquire into the condition and needs of displaced persons in Germany who may be stateless or non-repatriable, particularly Jews. I am sending you a copy of that report. I have also had a long conference with him on the same subject-matter.

"While Mr. Harrison makes due allowance for the fact that during the early days of liberation the huge task of mass repatriation required main attention, he reports conditions which now exist and which require prompt remedy. These conditions, I know, are not in conformity with policies promulgated by SHAEF, now combined displaced persons executive.

But they are what actually exists in the field. In other words, the policies are not being carried out by some of your subordinate officers.

"For example, Military Government officers have been authorized, and even directed, to requisition billeting facilities from the German population for the benefit of displaced persons. Yet, from this report, this has not been done on any wide scale. Apparently it is being taken for granted that all displaced persons, irrespective of their former persecution or the likelihood at their repatriation or resettlement will be delayed, must remain in camps—many of which are overcrowded and heavily guarded. Some of these camps are the very ones where these people were herded together, starved, tortured and made to witness the death of their fellow-inmates and friends and relatives. The announced policy has been to give such persons preference over the German civilian population in housing. But the practice seems to be quite another thing.

"We must intensify our efforts to get these people out of camps and into decent houses until they can be repatriated or evacuated. These houses should be requisitioned from the German civilian population. That is one way to implement the Potsdam policy that the German people 'cannot escape responsibility for what they have brought upon themselves.'

"We quote this paragraph with particular reference to the Jews among the displaced persons:

"'As matters now stand, we appear to be treating the Jews as the Nazis treated them, except that we do not exterminate them. They are in concentration camps in large numbers under our military guard instead of S.S. troops. One is led to wonder whether the German people, seeing this, are not supposing that we are following, or at least condoning, Nazi policy.'

"You will find in the report other illustrations of what I mean.

"I hope you will adopt the suggestion that a more extensive plan of field visitation by appropriate Army group headquarters be instituted, so that the humane policies which have been enunciated are not permitted to be ignored in the field. Most of the conditions now existing in displaced persons camps would quickly be remedied if through inspection tours they came to your attention or to the attention of your supervisory officers.

"I know you will agree with me that we have a particular responsibility toward these victims of persecution and tyranny who are in our zone. We must make clear to the German people that we thoroughly abhor the Nazi policies of hatred and persecution. We have no better opportunity to demonstrate this than by the manner in which we ourselves actually treat the survivors remaining in Germany.

"I hope you will report to me as soon as possible the steps you have been able to take to clean up the conditions mentioned in the report.

"I am communicating directly with the British Government in an effort to have the doors of Palestine opened to such of these displaced persons as wish to go there.

"Very sincerely yours,
"HARRY S. TRUMAN."